DBT Workbook For Adults

Develop Emotional Wellbeing with Practical Exercises for Managing Fear, Stress, Worry, Anxiety, Panic Attacks, Intrusive Thoughts & More

(Includes 12-Week Plan for Anxiety Relief)

By Barrett Huang

https://barretthuang.com/

befitting its nature. Trademarks mentioned are done without written consent and should not be considered an endorsement from the trademark holder.

Table of Contents

Preface

"Be kind to yourself, then let your kindness fill the world."- Minna So

My dad was a hoarder, and my mother had undiagnosed anxiety. As a child, I was understandably extremely anxious, living in an environment that felt chaotic and confusing. The unrest I felt as a kid shaped me into an adult who now has Generalized Anxiety Disorder (GAD) and Obsessive-Compulsive Disorder (OCD).

One of my earliest compulsions was to make sure I never stepped on any lines or cracks on the pavement because I felt something terrible would happen to me.

Obsessions, negative thoughts, and constant worrying can be debilitating, and I have felt all of them. That feeling of dread, like something terrible will happen, is wired deeply into my psyche.

I sometimes still think that if I don't double-check the stove, the entire house will burn down. I check that the tap is turned off by tapping it 2-3 times. I still triple-check the door to make sure it's locked when I leave, or my brain tells me someone will break in and steal everything. I live in a safe, gated neighborhood. You would think my rational brain would take over and set me straight—but it doesn't. It's a constant struggle.

In the past, I'd be so nervous approaching and talking to a girl I was interested in that I would hyperventilate. This is because my brain tells me she will laugh in my face and humiliate me. I know these thoughts are irrational and unlikely to happen, but my mind and emotions get the better of me at times.

Thanks to working with professionals and using anti-anxiety medication, I have improved my symptoms over time. But for me, anxiety never truly goes away.

I live with these conditions daily, but I manage them well with the right tools and support.

I've done cognitive behavior therapy (CBT) and dialectical behavior therapy (DBT), and I believe both are beneficial. This book is for those who have tried CBT and other methods and haven't found much help. We will significantly focus on DBT in this book since it was the method that changed my life. I hope this book helps you better understand your anxiety and acquire the tools you need to better manage and improve your condition as I have.

Today, I'm calmer, more level-headed, and capable of handling challenges better than before. I've run a successful online business and have self-published numerous bestselling books. Even though it can be stressful, and I still get anxious, it's more manageable now.

Our upbringing and environment play a huge role in how we react to situations. It's clear to me now that my family was a significant source of my stress and anxiety, and the way I was brought up resulted in my brain being shaped into this ball of anxiety. Once I got older, I realized that the things I experienced were not normal, and I needed to get away from the situation to improve my life and mindset. Once I left home and began traveling the world, everything changed for the better.

I traveled around Asia, to Thailand, Manila, and Hong Kong. During my travels, my eyes were opened to different ways of life. I witnessed poverty, corruption, injustice, and strife that I wouldn't have seen otherwise. Through these experiences, I began to realize how privileged my life was.

I met people who had no arms or legs and were begging for change. I imagined their life as miserable, yet every last one of them had a smile on their face. This made me realize that whatever I am anxious about in my life is likely not as bad as what they are going through. And so began my journey into healing myself and rebuilding my life.

One of the biggest goals of this book is to show you, dear reader, that you are not alone.

Millions of people suffer from varying degrees of anxiety disorders, and no two are the same. At times, the way you are feeling may make you feel very much alone, but you are not.

If you or someone you know is in crisis, resources are available to you. Call a trusted friend or family member, Google your local crisis line, and if those methods do not seem to be enough to support you at the moment, head to your nearest Emergency Department. Anxiety and panic are no joke, and you do not have to suffer alone.

If you're in a state where you're ready to take control of your anxiety, let's get into it. To get the most out of this book, I advise reading one chapter at a time and completing the exercises I have shared with you at the end of each chapter. You can then re-read sections until you feel you've mastered them.

Note that the 12-week workbook included does not have to be completed in 12 weeks. It is essential to work through each chapter at your own pace.

Like everything else, some days will be easier and more beneficial to you than others. And there are going to be times that you need a break. During those times—take a break!

Addressing anxiety and helping yourself can take a lot out of you. There will be times when you're faced with your past, faced with debilitating emotions, and faced with tasks that seem physically and mentally impossible to do at that moment. Believe me, I've been there, and I genuinely get it.

But here's my number one rule: **BE KIND TO YOURSELF**.

Say it out loud—**I WILL BE KIND TO MYSELF**.

Write it down on a sticky note, make it your desktop background or phone wallpaper, write it on your bathroom mirror; place it everywhere to remind yourself to be kind and forgiving to yourself.

Whatever got you to this point, whether it was childhood trauma like me or another trauma later in life, I'm so very sorry that happened to you. But please know this—you are not your trauma, and you are not a reflection of whoever raised you.

YOU ARE INCREDIBLE just to pick up this book and want to better yourself. Take some credit for your first step!

In the following pages, we will cover the basics of anxiety. Don't worry; we will not dwell on that too long. We will then discuss DBT and how to get the most out of it, the major task of setting boundaries, and then dive into some more specific diagnoses as they relate to anxiety.

We will go through some DBT exercises that I found particularly helpful in my journey. Even if you don't have specific diagnoses, I suggest going through the chapters and the exercises anyway. Someone who does not have OCD may still benefit from the DBT exercises included in that chapter. DBT can help anyone with anxiety and anxiety-related conditions, such as phobias, social anxiety, PTSD, and ADD.

THANK YOU for being here, and please know that **YOU ARE NOT ALONE**.

I often felt that I was struggling in this world alone in dealing with my anxiety, so I found tremendous inspiration in others' stories. Just the thought that people out there understood what I was going through helped me.

I sincerely hope this book helps you on your path to healing too.

Chapter 1: The ABCs of DBT

"Let go of what you can't control. Channel all that energy into living fully in the now."

- Karen Salmansohn

We all want to be happy and think positive thoughts all the time. In reality, life is hard. But please remember this: it's never as bad as you fear. In fact, one study has shown that 91.4% of our worries don't come true at all.[1]

Still, I understand you. Often, even though we know specific facts (like our fears won't likely come true), we still feel the way we do. I'm usually asked WHY I feel anxious, and frequently my answer would be, *"I don't know. It's just there."*

Like me, you probably feel a tidal wave of emotions when you're anxious. Before, when this happens, I get paralyzed, feel lost, and quite frankly, get stuck in the moment, or worse, spiral down into even more anxious thoughts.

ACCEPT the Tidal Wave

One of the things that I learned is to simply accept—and not fight—that tidal wave of anxious feelings. Why? Because waves come and go. So I started to cope by letting the tidal wave hit me... and then wash over me.

CHANGE to Move Forward

Another coping mechanism that has helped me is understanding and applying the word *perspective*. Whenever my mind gets polluted with fear and negative thoughts, I try very hard to imagine a different perspective or possibility.

For instance, say I'm at some party. I meet someone, we get into some small talk, and then the other person moves on. I would get very anxious about how that person thought of me. Did they like me? Did they think I was weird? Stupid? Too friendly? Not friendly enough?

To slowly divert my anxious thoughts, I'd start to think of other possibilities. *What else could be true?*

Perhaps the other person was also nervous about meeting someone at a party.
Perhaps the other person had a bad day, so they weren't in the mood to be chatty.
Perhaps the other person was just shy.
Perhaps they have anxiety too.

By looking at the SAME situation from a different angle, I slowly changed my thoughts and emotions about the event. No, it's not that there's something wrong with me; something else may be happening in that person's life.

ACCEPTANCE and CHANGE are the two strategies at the heart of dialectical behavior therapy.

What is Dialectical Behavior Therapy or DBT?

Dialectical behavior therapy (DBT) was developed by Marsha M. Linehan[2], Ph.D., in the 1980s as a result of her and her colleagues' work with patients with borderline personality disorder (BPD).

Working with BPD patients who were suicidal, Linehan realized that, unlike cognitive behavior therapy (CBT), which focuses primarily on detecting negative thought patterns and changing them to positive ones (change-focused), it is far more effective to employ two opposing (dialectical) strategies: acceptance AND change.

ACCEPTANCE   CHANGE

RADICAL ACCEPTANCE in DBT

DBT teaches people to accept their feelings, emotions, and realities AS IS without judgment.

You have a right to feel what you feel. Your emotions are valid. There's nothing wrong with you.

And there's no need to delve deeper into the source of your pain (or anxiety), figure things out, or pass judgment on yourself, other people, or the situations that may have caused your anguish. Doing this will just make you *stay* in that negative state and may *lead* you to an emotional (rather than logical) reaction that may worsen the situation.

➡️   It is what it is.

CHANGE in DBT

Acceptance comes with realizing that your current ways are not beneficial to you. As such, you recognize the importance of shifting your time, thoughts, and energy into learning new behaviors, skills, and techniques to help you cope better with life.

➡ It is what it is. I'm now going to learn new ways to positively move on.

DBT focuses on developing four (4) primary skills. None of these are easy to learn, but the benefits of *retraining your mind* can lead you to a more carefree and fulfilling life.

<u>The Four Pillars of DBT</u>

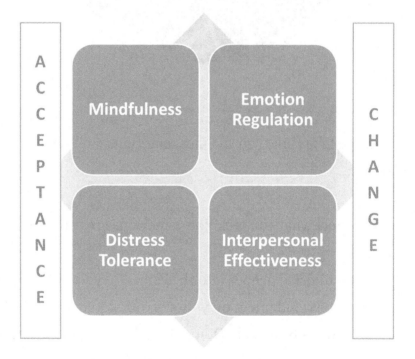

- **MINDFULNESS** is being aware of the present moment without judgment. It is observing, describing, and participating in the NOW. It can include narrowing your attention or focusing on something specific. Other times, mindfulness involves noticing the world around you or expanding your awareness.

- **DISTRESS TOLERANCE** is increasing your tolerance of negative emotions (as opposed to denying or trying to escape them) to improve the outcome of a stressful situation.

- **INTERPERSONAL EFFECTIVENESS** is improving your interpersonal skills to get more of your needs met while maintaining good relationships with those around you. It is about finding a balance between dealing with others without losing your self-respect.

- **EMOTION REGULATION** is managing negative and overwhelming emotions while increasing positive experiences. To regulate emotions effectively, it is crucial to understand that negative emotions are not necessarily bad or something to be avoided. Experiencing these feelings is a natural part of life, but there are ways to deal with them so they do not control us.

A trigger event activates automatic negative thoughts in people with anxiety who have high emotional sensitivity. As a result, these thoughts trigger an adverse emotional response, leading to destructive behavior choices. In the aftermath of detrimental behavior, shame and self-loathing become more prominent. Emotional regulation helps sufferers learn to cope with their emotions more effectively.

The purpose of DBT is to change the way you perceive the world and how you react to it because the way you are seeing the world right now is not working for you.

If you're in a constant state of anxiety, your fight-or-flight system is always ready to go. You're hypervigilant, and that sense of dread can be incredibly overwhelming, adversely affecting your physical health. Without getting too far down the biological rabbit hole, chronic stress negatively impacts your health and well-being.[3] So, it is in your best interest to learn and adopt the skills we'll cover in this book.

Here's what you will learn in the following pages:

1) **Acceptance Skills.** Learn strategies to cope with people, situations, and emotions in your life. Additionally, you will develop skills to help you improve your interactions and behaviors towards others.

2) **Behavioral Skills.** Discover how to become proficient at analyzing issues or destructive behavior patterns and replacing them with healthier and more effective ones.

3) **Set Boundaries.** Find out how to effectively set boundaries with family, friends, co-workers, spouse, and even yourself.

4) **Cognitive Skills.** Learn how to change beliefs and thoughts that do not serve you.

5) **Collaboration Skills.** Develop your communication and teamwork skills, which can help you with your relationships at home, work, or school.

6) **Support Skills.** This part will be directed toward developing and utilizing your positive strengths and qualities.

Conditions Mentioned in this Book

The content in this book has been broken down into various conditions and how DBT can help address them. Emotional regulation and self-destructive behaviors are prevalent in many mental health conditions, so although DBT has been initially developed for BPD patients, this type of therapy has broad applications[4].

DBT Worksheet Overview

This book includes a 12-week plan for anxiety relief. The goal is to help you begin a self-guided course where you learn to use DBT skills to cope with your anxiety. Most of these exercises are derived or adaptations from Marsha Linehan, Ph.D., the creator of dialectical behavior therapy (DBT).[2]

DBT is based on cognitive behavior therapy with a strong emphasis on mindfulness and emotion regulation. As such, you will learn tools for living in the moment, healthily dealing with stress and emotions, and improving your relationships with others.

The exercises are divided into the four primary DBT skills: Mindfulness, Interpersonal Effectiveness, Distress Tolerance, and Emotion Regulation.

As you move through this book, it's important to remember that you don't have to do these in order, and you can always go back and revisit any of the topics we've covered. This is your journey, and you are in charge.

One last thing before we really get going: some of the following content and exercises will challenge you in ways that perhaps you haven't been challenged before. You may get upset when thinking about or working through difficult subjects. Some of this may be related to trauma, but some could be difficult points you need to accept about yourself.

I just want you to know that it's okay to be upset. It's okay to take breaks. Remember my motto at the beginning of this book: **BE KIND TO YOURSELF**.

WORKBOOK: WEEK 1 - DBT Basics

As mentioned, dialectic behavior therapy (DBT) is about the coming together of two seemingly opposite (dialectic) strategies: Acceptance AND Change. This exercise will help you start practicing these core DBT concepts.

Exercise: Self-Acceptance and Change

I've put some sample statements here for you as a guide.

SELF-ACCEPTANCE:

DESIRE TO CHANGE:

YOUR STATEMENT:

This is difficult... but temporary.

I am not as happy as I know I could be.

"I accept myself as who I am right now. I know I'm like this for a reason even though I don't know exactly why. What I do know is that I don't feel happy or fulfilled living this way. I know this is not my best life. So I accept myself without judgement and I'm open to learning new things and exploring myself further to increase my happiness."

I AM DOING MY BEST. THAT'S ENOUGH.

I AM OPEN TO IMPROVING MY LIFE.

Things are not going as planned. That's

I know there are other parts of me I can explore to live

It's okay to feel this way.

I WILL NOT FEEL GUILTY FOR WANTING TO TAKE CARE OF MYSELF.

My feelings are valid.

There's nothing wrong with wanting 'more'.

Now, it's your turn...

Fill out the following diagram with your own Acceptance and Change statements.

Important: Don't put any pressure on yourself, ok? Just write whatever you feel. If nothing's coming to you today, that's ok too. You can always return to this exercise whenever it suits you.

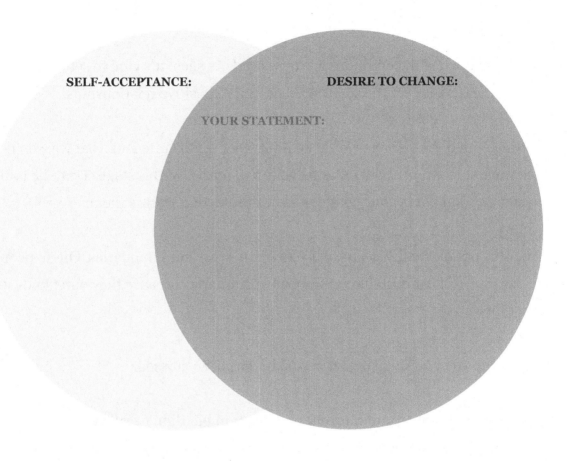

SELF-ACCEPTANCE:

DESIRE TO CHANGE:

YOUR STATEMENT:

Chapter 2: Boundaries – Self-Care 101

"Daring to set boundaries is about having the courage to love ourselves even when we risk disappointing others." - Brene Brown

Many mental health conditions are *triggered*. As such, it's vital to set healthy boundaries as they set the stage for healthy and positive relationships.

Setting boundaries is a way for us to limit what we tolerate and what we won't. I ask you not to stress about defining your boundaries at this stage. Truth be told, most of us don't know our boundaries until someone crosses them.

And let's not blame the people who currently cross our boundaries. Often, people in our lives feel comfortable crossing our boundaries because they don't know what they are.

So how do you know when your boundary has been crossed?

Have you ever done something out of obligation but didn't really want to? Has your happiness ever been sacrificed to keep peace in a situation where everyone else is happy? Have you ever gone along with someone or a group just because it was easier than saying and explaining what's on your mind? Has anyone ever commented on your body, intellect, choices, or life without any correction from you?

Reflect on at least one of my questions and think about how these situations made you feel. Not good, right?

But here's the thing, not speaking up for yourself will also make you feel "not good". Let's back up a little bit.

Setting boundaries begins with you. You need to decide what is important to you. No one else can figure that out.

For example, imagine saving your money as a young adult and moving into an apartment. Your parents come to help you move, and they criticize everything about the place: it's too far from work; it's too small; there's no bathtub (only a shower); on and on it goes.

Your parents make you feel small about your choices, so you fight, and they leave. A little deflating, right?

Trying to please everyone damages you in the end.

Most of us who identify as people-pleasers or peacekeepers don't want to upset the apple cart and are afraid of conflict. We spend a lot of time and energy managing the perceptions of others and taking more responsibility than is ours. We abandon ourselves to make sure that other people are okay instead of checking in with ourselves to see if we are okay.

To be happy and develop positive relationships, you must reclaim your power! Instead of giving everything away to everyone, including yourself, take care of yourself first by prioritizing what you need. And it begins with self-awareness.

Ask yourself: what do I want? What are my preferences?

Knowing what you want will help you put yourself and your needs first. Many people don't even ask themselves these questions, so you're already ahead of the game. This is how you become self-aware.

Also, if you don't decide what is important to you, others will make the decision for you. And guess what? Their choices are often not in your best interest but theirs.

The second step is to **communicate and express your preferences (boundaries)**.

It's not enough to know your boundaries; you should state them. If you don't, people will keep crossing that line. This is just how things are in life; people will push for what they want.

So despite how uncomfortable it may feel, express your honest opinions, thoughts, and feelings, even if you're scared the other person might get hurt. True, you might offend someone, but what is the worst that can happen?

We are often too afraid of hurting other people or getting into uncomfortable, awkward situations, so we tend to hold back. But who is that hurting and damaging in the end? I think you already know the answer to that one.

Boundaries with Family

Family dynamics are complex. If you were fortunate to grow up in a loving and supportive family and/or were raised in a peaceful environment where you felt heard and validated, congratulations! The majority of people did not.

From an early age, many people had their boundaries crossed. Think of the last time you visited your uncle or another relative, and you were ~~asked~~ told to kiss or hug him. In my family, a common thing is for relatives to ask whom I am dating and when I plan to get married. These questions can be intrusive, no?

When you were a kid, your parents may have crossed boundaries to protect other people's feelings. So you're taught early to "just be polite" or "just smile" and hug or kiss your relatives. One of the most common scenarios is when a parent crosses a child's boundary by not respecting their body autonomy. My point is that we learn early to break our own boundaries for the sake of others.

Growing up, we are taught to do things because Mom would like us to do them or because this will mean we are a good person. Yes, there has to be a balance between being a happy, giving, and loving person who wants to help other people and learning how to fill ourselves up inside and feed ourselves the love and acceptance we deserve.

Even as grown adults, most of us deal with boundaries and power struggles in dealing with older relatives. If you're a grown adult who lives alone or with a partner, and your parent(s) have a key to your home for safety reasons, and they hardly use it, fine.

However, how would you feel if they had a key to your home and showed up uninvited and unannounced? How would you react if they went through your stuff, rearranged the contents of your kitchen cabinets, and threw out all your snacks? How far do you think your parents crossed your boundary in this scenario? You know what? This is what my mom did to me!

What if your parent or loved one criticizes your appearance, lifestyle choices, or career? How would that make you feel? What if you go to your parents' house every Sunday night for dinner because it's a family tradition, and they tear apart your new haircut, outfit, and everything you bring up with them? Would you keep going back? This has been my experience, affecting my decision-making abilities throughout life.

Everyone in my family is super direct. There is no sugar-coating or political correctness here. On the one hand, it's good to have people who directly state how they feel. But if all you hear is negative criticism, it gets annoying, and it chips at your self-esteem.

Parents and relatives say that they do these things out of love. They care about you, so they want to 'correct' you. If you look pale, they say you should sleep more and work less. If you don't look healthy to them, they say you should lose weight (or gain weight). These things can hurt at the moment, and it's sometimes hard to remember that they say these things from a place of love. So it gets very confusing because, on the one hand, you believe this person loves you, but at the same time, they seem to see only your flaws. (Message: You're not good enough.) This is why I advocate setting boundaries.

If we don't set boundaries, the people who claim to love us, and often we love them back, are the ones who will slowly break us down in the end.

Establishing healthy boundaries is good and will give you more peace of mind. Otherwise, your future may consist of your parents determining your every adult decision and undermining your authority with your own kids. Setting those boundaries is going to serve you for a long time.

So, consider what you stand for, what you like, and where your morals are. Get to know yourself to discover your boundaries. Once you've realized that a boundary needs to be drawn, communicate it immediately.

For example, if your parents are overtly religious, and you are not, it's perfectly okay to say, *'Hey Mom and Dad, I love you, but I've decided not to attend church anymore. Organized religion just doesn't align with who I am.'* No explaining further, just a fact.

Your parents will likely have a massive issue with this. Take comfort in knowing that a) people do not like change; b) your parents see the time at church as a way to spend time with you and may feel rejected, and c) if they love you, they will eventually get over it.

Setting boundaries, especially if you've never done them before, isn't easy, and it's likely going to cause issues in your family. But if you want to set clear, healthy boundaries with your loved ones, this is a step you will have to take.

By the way, this doesn't mean that our parents set out to destroy our lives! Remember that our parents are doing the best they can with what they know. They're pretty much carrying over the parenting style of *their* parents.

The difference is that we know and acknowledge that we don't have to subject ourselves to the same rules and do the same things to our children.

Breaking cycles is part of setting boundaries. Your mom may insert herself where she does not belong, such as telling you how to parent, and it's up to you to protect yourself (and your children) when she does.

It's about seeing things from a more holistic point of view, which isn't easy. As I got older and did much self-reflection and gained a better understanding of my Chinese culture, I realized that my parents did the best they could with my sister and me.

They weren't perfect, but I know they love and care for us. I also realized that it wasn't fair to have Western expectations of them. For example, I yearned for them to say '*I love you*' and express their feelings as they do here in North America. But that's not the Chinese family culture. At the same time, though, they had to realize that we are not in China anymore and should respect my feelings and beliefs.

Hopefully, having an honest conversation with your parents helps you better understand each other.

Please remember that as you communicate who you are to them, try to understand them too. Ask *them* about *their* stories. Ask *them* about *their* feelings. Ask *them* about *their* life journey.

For me, taking a course in Chinese history and learning about how my parents grew up were some of the best things I did. It helped me understand where they were coming from and exercise more patience with their ways.

Boundaries with Friends

It's human nature to want to be accepted by our peer groups. When making friends, we tend to be on our best behavior, and some of that includes sacrificing our own needs for the sake of others. No question about it, our parents and society have conditioned us to put other people first. And I think that's where it gets a little twisted.

We focus so much on giving in to other people's wants that we neglect ourselves.

As kids, something as simple as being on the playground and being told to share something makes you share because it's the right thing to do. When making friends, we're told that we should be nice so that others will like us. And often, being friendly means going with what other people like and do.

No one teaches us that thinking of ourselves and sticking to what we like and do is okay.

Of course, it's important to teach children how to share. But on the other hand, maybe the first child just started playing with the ball and the second child needs to learn to wait their turn. Or perhaps both children need to learn how to play ball together. There's a balance that is missing.

When we get older, in adolescence or adulthood, we still want that feeling of belonging. For example, let's say you're with a group of friends and 8 out of the 10 enjoy camping, while the other two despise it. Now, these two tell a joke that they would rather not spend their money living in filth and sleeping on the ground. The rest of the group then pressures these two by saying something like, *"Oh, but it will be fun! Just you guys wait and see"* or *"But it won't be the same without you guys!"*, or worse, *"If you guys aren't going, we're not going."*

What do you think will happen? Most likely, the two anti-camping friends would give in and join because of peer pressure. But what *should* happen is that the pro-camping friends should respect those who don't want to join and that the anti-camping friends should stick to their choices. This is what true friendship is all about.

Now, if you have a friend that puts you down consistently, yells at you, and calls you names, that's a big problem. This is where you should stand up for yourself, right? That's obvious.

But what if you DO stand up for yourself and your friend calls you over-sensitive, selfish, or even stupid? This pushback may shock you, but please expect it if you've never stood up for yourself before.

Once *pushback* happens, would you start questioning yourself and wonder if you are too sensitive or selfish? Would you back down to keep the peace? If you do, what would that make you feel? Don't you think that standing up for yourself and backing down would make your friend respect you more? On the contrary, this move will *empower* your so-called friend not to take you seriously next time.

So what do you do? Establish your boundaries, and if that means losing a few friends along the way, that's okay.

Even if you've been friends for 15 or 20 years, it's okay to want change. It's okay to want to be treated better. If this friend truly cares about you and isn't some psychopath, they will take the time to re-learn how to treat you.

If they are not receptive after your first few tries at setting boundaries, as difficult as it might be to say goodbye to this friend or distance yourself from them, it may be necessary. Surrounding yourself with people who respect you and your boundaries is vital to your health.

You don't have to be mean or rude all of a sudden to make your point; you just have to be firm and confident with what you are saying to protect yourself. It's said that we are the average of our five closest friends, so you want to surround yourself with people who will support and motivate you to become better.[5]

One book I recommend is "*When I Say No, I Feel Guilty: How to Cope, Using the Skills of Systematic Assertive Therapy*" by Manuel J. Smith. I read it back in university, and it helped me set boundaries with friends and family. It also showed me that it's okay to say no and not feel guilty when I don't want to do something others do. Although the book is a bit dated, there are plenty of tips and examples to help you become more assertive in your life.

I won't lie to you; conversations regarding boundaries will make you uncomfortable, but it's essential to stick to them. If a friend is exhibiting negative behavior towards you, tell them to stop and continue stating it until you lose that 'friend' or the negative behavior changes. I know it's hard and will take time, but doing this improves your relationship with others and the one you have with yourself.

Boundaries help improve our confidence and help get rid of some of the anxiety in our lives. It may be helpful to practice what you want to say beforehand, especially if you're nervous or prone to anxiety. If you are prepared for these moments, you will be strong when it counts.

Here are some example starter phrases for you.

> *I'm busy now, so please feel free to do [x] without me.*
> *I'm really not into [x], but you guys have fun!*
> *I tried [x], but I realized it's not really me, so I'm afraid I won't be joining you guys.*
> *Sorry, I can't help you with [x] because my plate is too full as it is.*
> *Thanks for the invite but I'd rather not go.*
> *Hey [friend], I've told you a couple of times before that I don't like it when you [x]. I'm uncomfortable with it, so can you please not do it?*

Yes, it can be exhausting and frustrating to constantly establish your boundaries, but it must be done. And when you do so, the best way is to do it assertively. Apart from the fact that assertiveness increases self-esteem and improves mental well-being,[6] being assertive implies to your friends that they should simply respect your and your wishes. (It's not open for discussion.)

Note that to be assertive is not to be aggressive. You're not in combative mode. Most simply and respectfully, you're just saying what your boundaries are.

Top 8 Tips for Establishing Boundaries with Friends

1. Mentally pump yourself up with positive self-talk. It may sound corny, but if you know you're going to have to stand your ground, try thinking, *'I can do this'* or *'This should be done'*, or *'This is for my mental health'*.

2. Practice the conversation ahead of time to reduce nervousness and the likelihood of you relenting. It's best to do this, whether out loud, before a mirror, or with a trustworthy confidante.

3. Setting your boundaries doesn't have to be verbal only. Be aware of what you are saying through your body language. When we want to please others, being assertive can be challenging, so when you have this conversation, be sure you're sitting or standing straight, your shoulders are rolled back, and you keep eye contact.

4. Feel free to share your *emotions* as you set your boundaries with your friends. Emotions will have more validity if they are expressed. In addition to increasing self-respect, acknowledging one's feelings also serves as a reminder that feelings matter. We create a bridge when we share our emotions and let others know what we're feeling.

5. Take responsibility for what you communicate. Don't accuse the listener since accusatory statements can put them on the defensive and make relaying your message more difficult. For example, you might say, '*I feel humiliated when you tell our other friends what happened to me last summer*.' The 'I' statements express how you are feeling.

6. If you receive a request that could endanger your wellbeing, Just Say No. An apology is not necessary, and it is best to clearly, respectfully, and honestly say 'no'. If you have just recovered from bronchitis, do not go skiing with your best friend. If you are unable to pay your own rent, do not lend your friend money.

7. Whenever necessary, concisely rephrase your words. People may find your boundaries challenging to understand and accept, primarily if you are exhibiting assertive behavior for the first time. However, boundaries should

not be negotiable. If someone questions you or shows hostility, repeat yourself firmly.

8. Talk to a therapist if you have difficulty communicating your boundaries. A therapist can identify the underlying factors that make it difficult for you to express what you need, and they can give you new methods of navigating these roadblocks.

Boundaries with the Digital World

Social media addiction and other online-related disorders are real, and many of these conditions include but are not limited to depression, loneliness, anxiety, sleep disturbances, and low self-esteem.

Our real lives are becoming more mixed with our online life, so we should set clear boundaries with digital tasks like email and social media. For example, if you finish work at 5 PM but still answer emails until 8 PM or 9 PM, that can indicate a problem. It's important to shut down your digital world at set times so that you can focus on other aspects of your life too.

Personally, I only check emails a couple of times a day, which allows me to reply to all messages at one time. This lets others know that they operate on my time and not the other way around. To this day, I haven't had anyone get angry with me for replying to a message or email the following day.

You're not the only one who experiences anxiety or stress over email! The inability to complete tasks (the feeling that you aren't accomplishing enough) is one of the most common triggers for social anxiety and productivity-related anxiety.

It's stressful to communicate by email because it's asynchronous, sending messages before receiving replies. We don't know when we will hear back.

A significant amount of context, tone, and emotion is also missing from emails. Email is often perceived as confusing and anxiety-inducing due to these factors.

Here are a few of the most common scenarios regarding email anxiety and what you can do to handle them.

1. **You are not receiving a timely reply from someone.** Our brains tend to make up stories to explain why we're not getting a response. Often, we think of social rejection. Did we say or do something to offend the other? Are we not important enough to deserve a reply?

   In reality, this is not about you. Other people's email behavior is about them and what's going on in their lives at that moment.

   So when someone does not reply to your email, don't take it personally. It may not mean much if a friend or colleague doesn't respond to you. Some people are so overloaded with emails that they cannot reply to all of them right away, even if they want to.

   So what do you? Keep a record of times when you have been frustrated by a slow response, and then it turned out you were worried about nothing. As these incidents occur, keep a running list. A great way to convince your brain that you shouldn't be anxious over slow responses is to collect data directly from your own life.

2. **Lack of effusiveness in emails.** Email communication lacks tone of voice and body language, so many people resort to exclamation points and smiley faces to make up for it. In an email, anxious people sometimes worry that the absence of clear emotional signals can indicate something is wrong, and it is not necessarily true.

Those with an anxiety disorder are more likely to see negativity or hostility when none exists, so keep some balancing self-talk ready when you notice this reaction.

For example, consider other possibilities. What *else* could be true?

- Perhaps the responder isn't very expressive over emails.
- Maybe the responder was tired, distracted, or in a hurry while writing their response.
- Perhaps the responder was unsure if you were okay with a casual conversation over email, so they used a more formal and direct tone.
- Maybe something bad happened that day to the other person, so they were not in the mood when they responded to you.

Look, you'll most likely never find out what happened. And because of that, email is often anxiety-provoking but know that 'not liking you' is often NOT the reason for an email that lacks enthusiasm.

So what do you do? Re-read the email; perhaps your anxious state when reading it caused you to miss any positivity present in the email.

Whenever I talk about anxiety-driven thinking, I usually refer to certain biases we have as 'cognitive blind spots'. When this occurs, we tend to miss positive signals entirely, and instead, we fixate on anything that appears negative or ambiguous.

As mentioned at the start, I have Generalized Anxiety Disorder (GAD), so this pattern of negative thinking happens to me a lot, making me overreact or perceive negativity when it isn't there. However, since I know my biases, I use the *What Else Is True* strategy I described here, which is very beneficial!

3. **You worry about email overload.** When your inbox takes up so much of your time and energy, it makes you feel anxious and frustrates you when you can't get to meaningful work.

So what do you? Monitor the time you spend e-mailing with a timer or an app. Do this for about a week to see how much time you email on average. From there, try to spend 5% to 10% less time on email each week to avoid getting overwhelmed. How? Writing shorter emails is one way to achieve this. Another tip is to separate important and less important emails and reply only to the important ones first. If you have more time, only then do you get the time to respond to the less important ones.

Also, try not to be too hard on yourself. Individuals with differing schedules don't always expect a response to emails sent in the evening or during the weekend. It might be an unnecessary psychological pressure you're placing on yourself if you feel the need to respond to emails over the weekend or late in the evening.

You can also ask others for advice. See what other people are doing to solve their email overload problem. Family, friends, and coworkers are likely facing the same problem as you, so ask if anyone has advice on how to handle this.

Then there's that giant time suck: **social media**.

Social Media's Contribution to Our Anxiety

Comparing ourselves to others is in our nature.[7]We do it all the time: we compare our current situation to our previous situation, our current self to our old self, ourselves to others our age, and our knowledge and abilities to others in our niche.

However, in the online world, we compare our realities to an *illusion*, specifically an illusion of the perfect life.

People say they don't care about the images they see because they know they are edited. Still, they admit to using several filters on their pictures every day and taking multiple photos from different angles before choosing which ones to share. We want to put out our 'best selves' and 'best life' because when others see our social media feeds, we don't want to be judged as 'less'.

Sharing snippets of our life in pictures and text is not without purpose. What are we hoping to achieve? We want people to like us, and the absence of approval or validation in the form of likes, positive comments, and re-tweets can lead to low self-esteem, body image issues, and self-consciousness. Numerous studies have also linked social media to anxiety and depression.[8]

FoMO, or Fear of Missing Out, is a phenomenon that has been worsened by social media, with a reported 69% (7 in 10) of millennials experiencing it.[9] With FoMO, you're always checking what your friends and followers are doing because you don't want to miss out. You want to know what they know. You want to do what they do.

People who have FoMo report feeling anxious, lonely, and inadequate. The most common example is when you notice friends at a particular location (because they have their GPS location turned on), and you are not invited.

Those who don't have a strong social media presence may still experience an anxiety condition called *nomophobia* or Fear of Being Offline (FoBO).

We are constantly distracted by the *beep*, *buzz*, and *ding* of our devices, yet we're addicted to hearing them. This is because every time we respond or get a notification that someone liked, commented, or re-tweeted something about us, our brains release dopamine, a neurotransmitter that's also called the 'pleasure chemical'.[10]

So if the presence of notifications boosts our moods, the opposite is also true; their absence deflates us.

Of course, not all notifications elicit positive emotions. For example, people become even more anxious and depressed if they receive notifications about their former partner and their new love interest.

So what do you do? I suggest you cut down on your social media use, especially if you notice that it's affecting your quality of life and contributing to your anxiety.

Top 6 Ways to Limit Social Media Use

1. Resist the urge to share everything. Enjoy an evening with friends for the sole purpose of being with friends, not to have an opportunity to snap something and post it on social media. Live in the moment and concentrate on those around you.

2. If you spend most of your time checking other people's accounts, limit the number of platforms you use on social media.

3. Turn off notifications. Disable or limit push notifications for social media or enable the Do Not Disturb mode on your mobile device. Trust me, that FoMO feeling you may have now will dissipate. After a couple of days, you will wonder why you ever had your notifications on in the first place. It's much more peaceful without them!

4. Take frequent digital timeouts during the day. Use apps to control your screen time or set the amount of time you plan to spend on social media. My limit is 20 minutes a day. I set a timer, and once that timer goes off, I shut down my social media apps.

5. Take a digital day off. Set one day in the week when you're off the grid. If you're a frequent poster, liker, or commenter, let family and close friends know so that they don't worry.

6. Go on a digital detox. Don't participate in social media for at least seven days. This will rehabilitate your brain from craving it. Out of sight, out of mind.

A word of caution: Sometimes, people are active online because of a sense of belonging and self-importance. If you go offline for an extended period and no one notices, that's okay. Please remember that you're going offline to take care of yourself and get back in touch with the REAL world, so go ahead and do that. Visit your mom, call a friend to meet up for drinks or dinner, or be quiet and read a book or clean your house. REAL LIFE has so much to offer, so be an active part of it.

Note: If you can't go on a digital detox because you use social media for your work or business then set some boundaries so that your work and personal lives don't overlap. Here are a few tips:

a) Consider delegating social-media related work to staff, a team member or even hire someone to do your social-media tasks for you.

b) Limit your use of social media for work only. This means you shouldn't check them outside work hours, nor access them for personal use. If possible, have a separate work phone where you install work-related social medis apps, and be sure to leave that device at the office.

Boundaries with Work

Whether you are a surgeon or a garbage collector, you have career responsibilities, work hours to adhere to, daily tasks to perform, and co-workers to deal with. Some co-workers are incredibly helpful and are great to work with, while others may need a lesson in teamwork and/or professionalism.

If you're struggling to set boundaries in the workplace, let me help you with this section. We will break this down a little into three categories: **work time boundaries**, **workload boundaries**, and **boundaries with co-workers**.

Work Time Boundaries

Like most of the population, you have set working hours. These hours are set by your employer and are usually part of a contract or a collective agreement. The expectation as to when you start and end working is clear (unless you have a workplace culture that fosters flexible working hours).

I have a friend who was an administrative assistant and payroll clerk for a small excavating company owner. Her boss, let's call him Paul, would call her at all hours, way past her 9-5 schedule. He would call as late as 1 a.m. on a Friday or on various hours during weekends, even if he knew she was away visiting family or me.

He would expect her to answer whatever question was on his mind at the time. He would call her to pick up his kids. He would call her when he was drunk and having marital issues. He even had her book a trip for him and his mistress. Boundaries? What boundaries?

Eventually, my friend had enough. She quit her job, and guess what? He continued to call her for a solid month afterward. He had handed so much of his work and personal business off to her that he needed information on many issues like where to find a certain contract, the status of certain bills, etc. He even asked for the contact information of his own divorce lawyer!

When she explained the situation to me, she told me she didn't quit sooner because '*the crew wouldn't get paid on time*". She was worried that the men who worked for this guy wouldn't get their paychecks because no one knew how to do it. She even trained a new person at the job for a solid week after her scheduled exit date.

Bottom line, you need to set work time boundaries because if you don't, your life will be about taking care of someone else's life.

Workload Boundaries

When it comes to workload, don't accept it when a co-worker tries to dump their work on you. Some of these people are sly and might say something like, '*but you're so much better at it than me*'. That may well be the case, but don't be a victim of your kindness here. Remember that if you give in, you may always be this colleague's 'go-to person'.

And difficult as it may be, you need to set boundaries with your boss too. If you don't, the goalpost of your responsibilities will move further all the time.

Workload boundaries function in a variety of ways and serve many purposes. The first benefit is that they clarify everyone's responsibilities. They help us maintain our emotional and physical well-being, remain focused on our individual principles, and identify our limits. Further, having clear workload boundaries will enable us to work more efficiently and effectively.

Workplace Boundary Examples

Workplace boundaries can only be set if there are clear-cut rules, to begin with. This establishes accountability and leaves little room for blame or excuses. Employees should be able to answer the following questions:

- What's your work schedule?
- To whom do you report?
- What's the scope of your work?

With the above examples, you can set the following sample boundaries.

- What's your work schedule? Once you know...

  Boundary: No calls to your home.

  Boundary: No calls beyond work hours.

  Boundary: No reading or replying to emails or messages after office hours.

- To whom do you report? Once you know...

  Boundary: No to projects handed by others.

  Boundary: No to tasks co-workers want to pass on to you.

- What's the scope of your work? Once you know...

  Boundary: No to projects you cannot take on due to a full schedule.

Of course, projects evolve, and flexibility is also required in the workplace. But when you feel you are doing more than you should, it is time to speak out.

Workplace Interpersonal Boundaries

Working together effectively requires the establishment of good, motivating, and respectful interpersonal boundaries in employee-coworkers and employee-management relationships. Without them, there is a possibility of one side taking advantage of the other, or workplace bullying may occur in the worst-case scenario.

Here are some examples of workplace interpersonal boundaries you may want to adapt.

- To avoid your personal and workplace lives from overlapping, consider NOT adding colleagues to your social media accounts. (And don't follow them either!)

- You may want to avoid talking about your personal life or anything you don't feel comfortable sharing at work (e.g., important family events, your anxiety, your religion, your political beliefs, etc.)

- During disagreements with colleagues or managers, always advocate for respect. This means no one should be ridiculing or scolding others. Also, remember to focus on the *issue*, not the people you're disagreeing with.

- If possible, close your office doors to indicate you don't want to be disturbed or when you simply need some quiet time to focus.

- When receiving feedback, state clearly that constructive feedback is welcome, but negative criticism is not.

Work-Related Personal Boundaries

You may not realize it, but you may be contributing to your work anxiety by NOT setting work-related personal boundaries. Following are a few things to consider.

- Leave your laptop and any work-related files or documents at work so that you don't reach for them at home.

- You've informed co-workers that you don't want to be reached at home or beyond work hours. Still, someone calls. What do you do? Don't answer. **Note**: If you feel that not being available puts you in a situation where you don't get as much involved in a project or any work-related decisions, consider having these calls go to voicemail. However, when you do this, restrict the times you check them (e.g., only from 5-6 PM) and reply only to issues that truly cannot wait till the next workday.

- Take time off when you need it; it's your right as an employee, and you deserve it. A 2016 poll in the United States found that the average employee with the ability to take paid time off (PTO) only took about 16 days, leaving 662 million vacation days unutilized.[11] Don't feel chained to your desk. If you need a break to take care of yourself—take it.

- Work smart, not long. This means you may need to take a step back and re-evaluate how you work. Are you prioritizing the right tasks? Are you easily distracted by less productive issues? Are you taking on tasks you should delegate to others? Consider *how* you work and see if your current methods are serving you.

As always, the first step to setting boundaries is to know what is personally important to you. For example, if you want to focus on your physical health, that means ensuring you have time to do that. So you may want to set a personal work-related boundary regarding the time you leave work to have time to exercise before dinner.

So how do you establish clear boundaries work?

You may feel anxious about letting co-workers know what you like and don't like, but honestly, it's not as hard as you think. Communicate your boundaries one conversation at a time or as the need arises. For example, if you notice that lunch breaks are becoming political debate times, say simply that you prefer not to discuss your political beliefs at work and that you'd much rather have a peaceful lunch. If colleagues continue to do this, then remove yourself from the situation.

What do you do when people violate your boundaries?
Speak up right away. Imagine your boundaries as a 'No Trespassing' sign on a gate. When people ignore the sign and cross over, point to the sign and close the gate again.

Still, when someone does not respect your boundaries the first time, try to remain compassionate. Most people don't realize how their actions affect you, so let them know they crossed the line so they won't make the same mistake again. Use specific rather than personal explanations.

Don't speak from your perspective when discussing work boundaries. Instead of saying, *'I'm stressed'* or *'I have a lot to do'*, which sounds whiny, explain the reason for your boundary by stating how it will affect other projects, your clients, or your bottom line. For example, say something like, *'If I focus on X, I'll not be able to focus on Y.'*

Have a game plan. A person suffering from anxiety will be uneasy when a boundary is crossed. Often, the stress is not just about the boundary violation itself but about how to handle it. We don't want the conflict. However, I've found that one of the best ways to handle this is to have a plan. Think about how you will handle the situation. List down the step you want to take and visualize what will happen.

For example, suppose your boss sends you a dozen emails while you're on vacation when they know that you're away.

Think about the best way to handle such a situation.

Step 1: I'll create an Out of Office reply so that anyone who sends me a message while I'm gone knows that I will only reply by [date].

Step 2: When [date] arrives, and my boss asks me why I didn't reply, what should I say?

a) I've properly informed everyone before I left that I would be on vacation; I expected that people would respect that.

b) I don't work on weekends, let alone during vacation days. But please do let me know if there was anything unsatisfactory before I left.

By being prepared, you will be better able to handle conflict.

Boundaries with Co-Workers

How do you handle your co-workers' laundry list of issues? Let us count the ways.

- If you're new to the team and your ideas are being squashed by long-standing employees, set the boundary that you're not a pushover by asking *why* your idea won't work. Who knows, perhaps you will learn something from their expertise and feedback. But if their response is *'it just won't work'*, or *'we do it this way'*, then you know your ideas aren't the problem—it's them.

  You may choose to let it go the first time, but push back if it keeps on happening.

  Be ready to state your ideas a second time. If you have to get to the third time, state that you may have to bring your concerns to your boss. Most times, their claims are unfounded, and they will back down at this point. Be confident. Do not waver. Practice beforehand if you feel you need to.

- Workplace harassment or bullying is never to be tolerated. The first time this happens, make sure it's the last time by strongly stating your boundaries. If it happens again, collect evidence and present this to your supervisor or inform human resources.

  If you're having boundary issues with your supervisor or boss, here are a few tips on how to handle the situation.

  - **Be clear about the boundary being crossed.** It's important to be communicate clearly. For example: I value my time at home so please note that I don't answer emails after 7 PM.
  - **Be ready with a non-emotional response.** If your boss has a habit of adding tasks to your list, instead of saying, *"I'm overloaded!"*, say

"Just to clarify… if I do, 'B', then I won't have time for 'A', which you gave last week. Do you prefer this?"

In short, don't make the issue about you. Show your boss the 'bigger picture'. You can even add, *"I'll prioritize what you tell me but I'm almost done with 'A', just so you know"* or *"I'll prioritize what you tell me but I believe 'A' is needed by Monday."*

- If your boss is not getting the message and keeps on crossing your boundaries, then do as above, collect evidence and present this to your human resources department.

- Consider how much you want to share. Like it or not, you'll be sending a lot of time with your co-workers. And yes, sometimes, knowing each other as individuals (as opposed to just a colleague) means better teamwork.

So consider what you're willing to share. If you find the questions too invasive (e.g., Who are you dating? How's your married life? Do you go to church?, etc.), one question I have in my back pocket is: *why do you want to know?*

This usually tells the person asking that I'm finding their questions inappropriate, stopping them in their tracks. If they do not stop, feel free to repeat your question. They'll get the hint!

Everyone has a right to a stress-free work environment and fair treatment. If you don't feel comfortable where you're working, the first step is always to state your boundaries in a friendly yet firm manner.

Again, be ready to explain what is acceptable to you and *why*. People often set boundaries by saying, *'It's not OK to'* or *'I don't want you to'* without stating their reasons. When this happens, your listener may become defensive and more likely to challenge your boundaries. So when always state your WHY. For example, say something like, '*It's not OK to interrupt my lunch hour with projects because I use that time to collect my thoughts and plan the rest of my tasks in the afternoon.*'

Consider giving your audience clear options, too, such as, '*I appreciate your emails and calls, but I would appreciate it if you email OR I call you at the end of the day if your note is not urgent. Which would you prefer?*'

You should also mention project goals when setting your boundary. For instance, '*If I'm not always in meetings and answering emails, I can focus on our clients better, and we'll hit our quota easier for this month.*' This way, your co-worker gets the big picture and, in doing so, may understand and support your boundary faster.

When all else fails, think if quitting is an option for you. Life is too short to be working with people who don't respect your boundaries. If you don't find going to work enjoyable anymore and view the workplace as nothing but a place of stress, then you should really consider quitting for your mental health.

What should you do when co-workers respect your boundary?

Consider that your co-workers may not be used to some of your boundaries because they've never encountered them before. Further, remember that setting boundaries is also asking others to stop what they are doing for your benefit. So when colleagues change and respect your boundaries, don't forget to say 'Thank You'. Depending on the gravity of the boundary, you may even give a small gift or token of thanks or simply say, "*Hey, just wanted to say I appreciate you respecting my boundary. How about lunch on me?*'

Work boundaries shouldn't divide you from your colleagues. Communicated the right away, you'll find that it helps not just you but also others in establishing a healthy and productive work environment.

Boundaries with Your Spouse/SO

You meet someone. You fall in love. You decide to live with this person for the rest of your life. But sometimes, darn, this person is annoying!

Like any relationship, setting boundaries with your partner should happen at the beginning of the relationship. Still, if you're with someone for a long time already, that doesn't mean you can't set boundaries anymore. There's no deadline for setting boundaries.

For instance, suppose you don't like it when your partner comes home while you're sleeping and makes a lot of noise as they get into bed. Or perhaps they turn the lights too early in the morning, waking you up unnecessarily. Whatever is bothering you, you need to be able to talk about it.

Suppose you and your friends are out together and your partner starts to flirt with someone. Some couples won't be affected by this because they feel secure in their relationship, but this can be a big issue if you have insecurities or have been the victim of infidelity. Although your partner may interact with other people this way when they first met you, you're not comfortable with that anymore. And you need to effectively communicate this with your partner. Otherwise, you'll end up feeling resentment towards them.

Setting your boundaries doesn't have to mean a fight. Your relationship can be strengthened in the long run by letting your partner know about issues that bother you.

Stating your boundaries with your significant other (SO) can require more kindness than with anyone else in your life. This is because you're so entwined with each other's lives, feelings, thoughts, and hopes for the future, that you don't want to hurt their feelings.

You also have to consider that your partner has been raised differently, and what works for you may not work for them. For instance, maybe your partner doesn't enjoy onions, and so instead of putting them into your pasta sauce like you have your entire life, you suddenly need to change things because you're living with somebody you love. Respecting each other's boundaries, communicating each other's needs and wants, and listening well to each other are the basis of any healthy, long-lasting relationship.

This is why it's important to have a clear idea of what you want and don't want in a relationship ahead of time. I've met many unhappy people, yet they stay with their partners because they don't want to be alone.

My first relationship was a disaster because I catered only to my girlfriend's needs and neglected my own. In the end, she lost attraction and respect for me. The funny thing is that a year after we broke up, she was attracted to me again since I had matured a lot. However, I was a different person and knew that she wasn't the right person for me.

I strongly advise you spend time thinking about what you want in a partner and write it down on paper. Think about the most important qualities that you want and don't want so that when you are dating someone, you can filter out people who are a terrible match for you. Knowing what you want is key!

Establishing relationship boundaries can be done in a variety of ways. To get you started, here are some suggestions.

1) **Start early.** Boundaries are much easier to establish at the beginning of any relationship than later because you're both emotionally invested and have established habits and routines by then.

2) **Communication is key.** It's important to remember that setting your boundaries should NOT be a one-way conversation. That's just asking for a fight.

   Start by timing your conversation right. For instance, don't start this when your partner has just woken up or spring this conversation at the end of their day when you know they're tired and stressed. Choose your moment and then say something like, '*Babe, can we sit down and talk?*'

3) **Use 'I' statements.** The way you say something is more important than what you say. So start with statements like '*I feel*' or '*I think*' or '*I am*'. If you begin with an accusatory statement such as '*You always*' or '*You never*', you will be met with '*I don't want to*'.

   Remember, nobody wants to be rejected or criticized, and getting back on track can be difficult once defensive barriers arise. You should strive to set boundaries with kindness based on how you wish to be treated.

   Also, always state the reason for your boundaries. For example, '*Babe, I am a light sleeper, so when you get into bed noisily, I wake up and have a hard time falling asleep again, making me groggy in the morning. I am just asking you to be mindful of that when you get into bed. Is that okay? Does that sound reasonable to you?*'

   Even though it's a 'boundary' for you, you must get their opinion on this so that your statements don't come across as a command.

Also, be specific with what you want or need. For example, your boundary is that you want one night a week to be alone, study, or read. If you're specific about why you need this alone time, your partner will receive it a lot better than if you say, *'Can you just leave me alone Thursday nights?'*

Asking for space is okay.

Regardless of how short or long you are in your relationship, know that it's okay to want to have some space. For example, you may need to decompress for half an hour if you have a demanding job when you get home. But instead of saying, *'Can you just leave me alone?'*, isn't it more beneficial to say, *'Babe, I just need 30 minutes when I come home to shift my mind from work. I'll be more useful to you and the kids that way. So when I come home, I'll be moving my ass to the offices first, okay?'*

The important thing is to explain that your request isn't a rejection of your partner. It's just something you need for yourself.

Keep in mind that things change.

Every relationship is different, and everything is flexible. During your relationship, there can be events that cause boundaries to shift, including:

- Becoming a parent.
- Moving into a new home.
- Getting a new job.
- Losing a loved one.
- Making new friends.

So even though a boundary has been stated, keep in mind that there should be room for change, development, and growth

Boundaries with Self

Lastly, let's talk about boundaries we should have with ourselves.

I'm currently transitioning to a work-at-home position, and I am guilty of rolling over and grabbing my phone first thing in the morning. Because of this, I start my day with my brain already churning before my body is even caffeinated.

So, I'm developing a morning routine that includes meditation and yoga so that I don't start my day with stress and demands. Carving out this 'ME time' takes some discipline, but I know it's for my own good, so I make the necessary changes.

For example, I have replaced my phone alarm with a traditional clock. This enables me to leave my phone in my office to charge overnight so that I don't get a chance to start checking my emails the minute I wake up.

Before I even set foot in my office, I start with some coffee, do about 30 minutes of stretching and meditating, and 5 minutes of journaling which includes a grateful practice.

In doing so, I start my workday feeling prepared mentally and physically. My goal is to increase this morning routine to a 60-minute routine where I walk first, stretch, and journal.

Some days, it takes more willpower to avoid my phone because I know emails are waiting from overseas clients who expect an answer before going to bed.

BUT...

My inner peace, mental focus, and physical well-being are more important than any client. I refuse to work before 8:30 AM. This mindset serves me well, but I'm still developing it, and the temptation to dive right into work is there almost every day. Creating these boundaries with myself serve me well in establishing discipline and protecting myself from burnout.

So I urge you to ask yourself these questions.

- *In what ways can I care for myself that I'm not currently doing?*
- *Are there needs in my life that I'm ignoring for the benefit of other people?*
- *What do I want to do if I had a FULL DAY all to myself?*
- *What do I want to do if I had a FULL WEEK all to myself?*
- *What new habits have I been thinking about that I just don't have time for now?*

Write down your answers on a sheet of paper. Analyze them. Are they really not doable? Chances are, THEY ARE. And if they're not ALL doable now, I guarantee there will be at least a few things you can do starting today. It's just that you haven't prioritized yourself before and set boundaries with yourself.

If you've been telling yourself, '*I really need to lose a little bit of weight*' or '*I should really get some good-quality sleep*', now is the time to set some of these self-care and self-love goals that need to happen.

You can set a deadline for yourself to get you to commit to your goals. For instance, I used to work until 10 or 11 at night. Now, I stop working at 7:30 pm. Then I work out, eat dinner, listen to an audiobook, and relax for the rest of the night.

I suggest you start by trying to establish a morning routine. Science says that it's extremely beneficial to making us more productive and less stressed during the day.[12]

Start with small changes, and don't shock your system. For example, if you wake up at 8 AM, set the alarm for 7AM and then give yourself about 20 minutes each day where you can't be disturbed. This time is only for you, and you can do anything you want.

Life is too short to work yourself to the point where your body shows signs of stress. Your anxiety levels will decrease if you take the time to care for yourself and love yourself the way you deserve to be cared for and loved.

Setting boundaries is one of the most important ways you can practice self-care. If you don't set boundaries with yourself and the people around you, you'll find yourself running on empty soon because you will give and give and give... until there's nothing left.

Communicating boundaries does not mean you're selfish. It just means you're not self**LESS**.

Many people are concerned that setting boundaries means losing relationships. On the contrary, my friend, it means establishing better and stronger relationships with people who really care about you. And if you lose someone, that's okay. Any person who doesn't respect your boundaries will only contribute to your anxiety or any mental health issue you may have.

So, protect yourself. Identify and communicate your boundaries. Define your space and look after your mental well-being, and you will be rewarded with better relationships.

WORKBOOK: WEEK 2 - Setting Boundaries

Boundaries are personal 'No Trespassing' signs you raise to promote your well-being and help ensure that we are not affected by others' actions and behaviors.

Although boundaries aim to protect you, you should ensure that you set **HEALTHY BOUNDARIES** and not unhealthy ones.

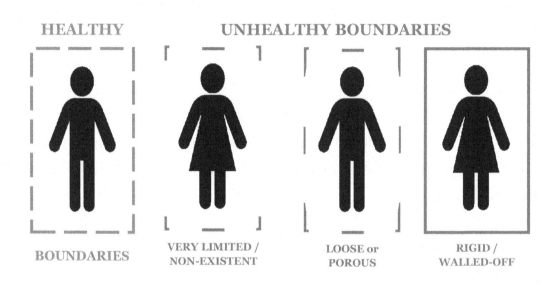

With the above in mind, please do the following exercise.

It indicates different types of boundaries and what they mean. Note there may be other boundaries you want to set that are not covered in the diagram (e.g., financial, internal spiritual, etc.) If so, then please feel free to add them to below or to a separate **My Personal Boundaries** sheet.

Remember, there are no right or wrong statements here.

All you need to do is consider what YOU want.

Exercise: Setting YOUR Boundaries

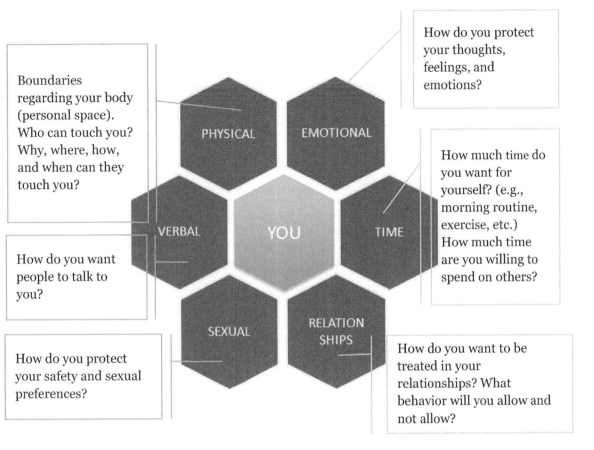

How do you protect your thoughts, feelings, and emotions?

Boundaries regarding your body (personal space). Who can touch you? Why, where, how, and when can they touch you?

How much time do you want for yourself? (e.g., morning routine, exercise, etc.) How much time are you willing to spend on others?

How do you want people to talk to you?

How do you protect your safety and sexual preferences?

How do you want to be treated in your relationships? What behavior will you allow and not allow?

Write your personal boundaries below. If necessary, get another piece of paper, label it your **My Personal Boundaries** and lay it all out there.

Physical Boundaries:

1.)

2.)

3.)

Verbal Boundaries:

1.)

2.)

3.)

Sexual Boundaries:

1.)

2.)

3.)

Emotional Boundaries:

1.)

2.)

3.)

Time Boundaries:

1.)

2.)

3.)

Relationship Boundaries:

1.)

2.)

3.)

Exercise: Boundary Journaling

If you're struggling to set and maintain boundaries, then you may want to sit down and make some notes about why and with whom you're having trouble setting boundaries with.

Take note of your feelings. Is someone or something triggering these emotions? Write everything down.

Next, answer this question: *what else is true*? This will give you a new perspective on the situation, and you may begin to see the person or circumstance differently as a result. If you feel a boundary has been crossed, develop a game plan on how to address the person or issue causing your distress.

STEP 1. Pick an area in your life making you anxious now.

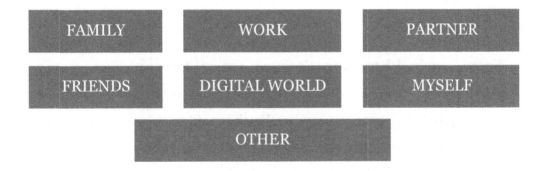

STEP 2. What are you feeling? (You can choose more than one.)

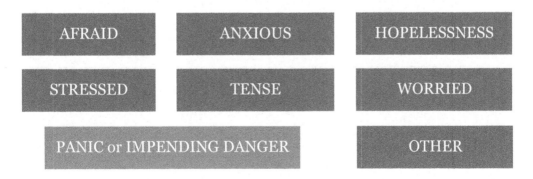

STEP 3. Is a specific person or event making you feel this?

Your answer: _____

STEP 4: Which boundary is being violated? (You can choose more than one.)

PHYSICAL	EMOTIONAL	VERBAL
TIME	SEXUAL	RELATIONSHIP

OTHER

STEP 5: Describe, in the simplest of words, the current situation. Example:

> **Area:** Family || **Emotion:** Stressed, Tense|| **Person:** Mom
> **Statement:** Mom called and is demanding I attend Sunday dinner and make up with my brother. My brother has told me – over lunch! – that he doesn't value me at all and wouldn't mind no further contact with me.

Your turn:

_____

_____

_____

_____

STEP 6. What else is true?

Example: Mom just really wants me to attend Sunday dinner because we haven't seen each other in over a month.

Your turn:

_____

_____

_____

_____

STEP 7: List down how you can re-instate your boundary.

Example: Mom, I love you, but I will not attend Sunday dinner. I need time to process how I feel about [brother] because he really hurt me. I will see you next Sunday.

Your turn:

Option #1.

_____

_____

_____

Option #2.

_____

_____

_____

Option #3.

_____

_____

_____

Chapter 3: Anxiety, Stress, and Worry

"Anxiety is like a rocking chair. It gives you something to do, but it doesn't get you very far."

- Jodi Picoult

The following is a story from a friend, KR:

When I was pregnant with my first child, I read every book I could get my hands on about pregnancy and babies. The books brought me knowledge, but they also made me a what-if monster. I constantly worried that I was gaining too much weight and causing a problem for my baby. I fretted over if I would be capable of caring for a baby properly. My mother hadn't been the best example, so I was determined to be the Best Parent in the World.

When the baby came, he was a happy, healthy little guy, and soon after he was born, he became very ill with a disease that had nothing to do with anything we had done as parents. Still, I wracked my brain over things I could have done differently to prevent an unpreventable disease.

For years after he recovered, I continued to worry excessively. I once asked my doctor if it was normal to keep my hands locked on my kids at all times while in public. I was hypervigilant about cars, strangers, foods, trampolines; you name it – everything was a danger, and I was a Mama Bear, ready to strike if anything came for my cubs.

In my 30's, my doctor sat me down, and we talked about my fears. I was then diagnosed with an anxiety disorder. I received medication, learned coping strategies to care for myself, and I can confidently say that I am now able to walk into a store with my now 23-year-old son and not worry that he might get hit by a car.

In fact, he's traveled the world with my blessing, starting at age 16! Thanks to my doctor recognizing that I needed help with my anxiety, I and my son both lead healthier lives.

Many different circumstances in our life can lead to anxiety, stress, or worry. It's normal to experience anxiety on the first day at a new job, on your wedding day, or when you're about to sign the closing papers on your first house. It's when anxiety interferes with your day-to-day functioning that you should evaluate your situation and speak to a health professional.

You are not alone if you're feeling overwhelmed and anxious, and you shouldn't feel shame in seeking professional help. Some of the signs that you need to watch for are:

- You no longer enjoy the things that you once did.
- You avoid situations that you once enjoyed, like socializing.
- You use alcohol or drugs to get through unpleasant situations.
- You experience one or more of the following:
  - A preoccupation with irrational fears and excessive worry.
  - Inability to fall or stay asleep.
  - Panic attacks.
  - Feeling too hot or cold.
  - Feeling restless, agitated, or irritable.
  - Weakness, dizziness, shaking, etc.

- Digestion problems.
- Chest pains.
- Difficulty focusing.
- Increase in heart rate.

A doctor can help you evaluate whether your anxiety is acute or transitory or whether you have an anxiety disorder. The following is a sample self-assessment form a professional may pose.

SELF-ASSESSMENT STATEMENT	Never	Sometimes	Most of the Time	All the Time
I find myself unable to sit still.				
I worry about several things at once.				
I am restless, agitated, skittish, or irritable.				
I am unable to feel calm or relaxed.				
I am unable to let go of feelings of fear or anxiety.				
I have been feeling moody and upset.				
I feel dread or feel that something terrible may happen to me or others.				
I have difficulty concentrating.				
I have difficulty getting to sleep and/or staying asleep.				
I have muscle tension.				

If you find yourself answering a good number of these points with *Most of the Time* or *All the Time*, professional help is advised.

Types of Anxiety

Mild anxiety is a sense that something is not quite right and that something needs extra scrutiny. Stimulating the senses will help you focus, which aids in learning, problem-solving, acting, thinking, and feeling better.

Note that mild anxiety is not always a bad thing. People are often motivated to change their behaviors or work toward a goal when mildly anxious. For example, students who are anxious about their exams can use that nervousness to concentrate better and develop better studying habits.

Moderate anxiety is when a person feels agitated over something (or someone) to the point that their sole focus is on the stressful situation. For example, say that you have a doctor's appointment. You might experience a faster heartbeat, stomach cramps, dry mouth, or even nausea over the appointment. When trying to explain the purpose of the appointment to others, you may talk faster than you normally do, make nervous hand gestures, or even bite your nails. These all point to the fact that your singular focus is the upcoming doctor's appointment.

When the date arrives, and your doctor gives you a clean bill of health, all your anxious symptoms subside.

Severe Anxiety is when a person panics to the point where all their survival skills become more primitive, defensive responses are initiated, and cognitive abilities sharply decline.

For instance, a person with severe anxiety who has suddenly been laid off from work may experience severe chest pains, vomiting, body shakes, scattered thoughts, and an extreme sense of dread over the future.

With severe anxiety, your ability to concentrate and find solutions is drastically impaired, which may lead to even more anxiety. You may not even be able to take care of your own needs, such as getting out of bed or eating on time. Attempts by loved ones to assist you are likely to be futile because you cannot move on from the stressful situation.

Types of Anxiety Disorders

People with anxiety disorders develop maladaptive behaviors and emotional disabilities because anxiety does not signal danger or prompt any motivation for change. Instead, the anxiety has become chronic, taking over their lives.

There are many manifestations of anxiety disorders. Following are some types.

Generalized Anxiety Disorder is characterized by persistent and excessive worry and anxiety for at least six months. During these events, you may experience uncontrolled worrying, significant distress, or social or occupational functioning impairment. In addition, you may suffer from restlessness, fatigue, difficulty concentrating or going blank, irritability, muscle tension, and sleep disturbances.

Panic Disorder is a state in which a person has reoccurring panic episodes. A panic attack is a brief period of acute dread that results in strong bodily symptoms such as hyperventilation, sweating, hot and cold flashes, trembling, rapid heart rate, inability to gather thoughts and speak coherently, feeling detached from reality, etc. Many people experience a panic attack once or twice in their lives. If you're experiencing more frequent panic attacks and find yourself constantly worrying about your next likely panic attack, you may be dealing with a panic disorder.

Social Anxiety Disorder (SAD) is a condition wherein a person experiences extreme fear in social settings. People with this disorder are afraid of being judged by others, so they avoid meeting people and attending social gatherings at all costs. Avoidance becomes their default behavior. Unfortunately, avoidance can make SAD worse because instead of learning coping mechanisms, the resulting isolation makes them even more anxious the next time they're in a social setting.

Obsessive-Compulsive Disorder (OCD) is a state in which a person experiences repeated undesirable views or emotions (obsessions) or the need to perform something again and again (compulsions). Most people with OCD recognize that their obsessions and/or compulsions are excessive and unreasonable, but they can't help but give in to them. Left untreated, it is almost impossible to ignore, suppress, or neutralize obsessions with compulsions. (For more details regarding OCD, please see Chapter 7: OCD & Compulsive Behaviors.)

Acute Stress Disorder is a condition wherein a person experiences a powerful and negative reaction to a traumatic event. Symptoms include feelings of intense fear, helplessness, hopelessness, horror, significant distress, or impaired functioning. There must be at least three of the following symptoms to make a diagnosis: (1) emotional detachment, (2) reduced awareness, (3) derealisation, (4) depersonalization, and (5) dissociative amnesia (inability to recall important aspects of the event).

Acute Stress Disorder can last from two days to four weeks. If you're experiencing this longer than this period, you may have post-traumatic stress disorder.

Post-Traumatic Stress Disorder (PTSD) is a condition that's caused by exposure to a traumatic event that involves intense fear, helplessness, or horror.

With PTSD, the person can't help but re-experience or re-live the traumatic event no matter how hard they try to get past it. It typically begins within three months to years after the event and may last a few months or years.

PTSD symptoms include intrusive recollections or dreams, flashbacks, and physical and psychological distress over reminders of the event. Avoidance and disassociation become a PTSD sufferer's recourse. For instance, this person may not want to see or talk to anyone associated with the traumatic event. Character changes are also common such as increased irritability, sudden and unprovoked angry outbursts, hypervigilance, exaggerated startle response, etc. (Please see Chapter 6: PTSD and Panic Disorders for a more detailed explanation of this condition.)

A **Phobia** is when a person experiences severe anxiety over a specific object or situation, which often results in avoidance (of that stimuli). Typically, phobias do not arise due to past negative experiences; you may have a phobia over something you've never encountered before.

Many people who have a phobia over something know that their fear is unusual and irrational, and they may even joke about how silly it is. Despite this, however, they feel powerless to stop their fear of it.

According to behavioral theorists, anxiety is mostly obtained from experiences. So if you *learned* anxiety, you could unlearn it by the same token. And one of the concepts related to this is *learned optimism*.

Learned Optimism

Two hamsters were placed in two separate cages. Hamster 'A' was given light electric shocks, but there's an option to escape the cage and move to another where there are no shocks. He tried; he succeeded and has moved to the shock-free cage.

Hamster 'B' was also subjected to light electric shocks, but unlike Hamster 'A', there were no ways to escape his cage. It becomes clear to 'B' that he has no control over the situation. His only option is to sit and accept the shocks.

After some time, hamsters 'A' and 'B' were removed from their cages and placed in two separate brand new cages. Both cages provided the option of escape. What do you think happened?

After the first light electric shock, 'A', knowing that he was able to escape the first time, quickly moved his ass and escaped. 'B', however, stayed put after receiving the first shock. He didn't even try. He was *conditioned* to accept the poor treatment. This is called *learned helplessness*.

Learned optimism is the opposite of learned helplessness. It's a concept developed by Martin Seligman[13], who's considered the father of positive psychology. It's the idea that you can learn to be optimistic and happy by challenging negative self-talk and replacing them with positive ones.

If you think that this is easier said than done, I can confirm that it is.

Happiness, optimism, and positivity are views that I personally need to keep on cultivating. You see, as a kid, I hated my life.

Anxiety and depression were my constant companions. I longed for that happy, normal family like what I saw on TV. Instead, my childhood was filled with anxiety. I was constantly worried about doing something wrong and making my dad angry. My parents' constant fighting (and eventual divorce) always made me nervous, stressed, and worried.

As I got older, I would complain a lot. I was always negative about everything—the eternal pessimist. In my mind, there was never any hope of things improving.

Truth be told, I probably learned that from my mother, who always played the victim card and never took responsibility for her actions. So I, too, always thought that life was just something happening to me. I'm the victim here since I have no control over anything.

After a lot of self-reflection and many attempts at working on myself, I finally started to heal. As mentioned earlier, taking the step to understand my parent's life stories and culture also helped me. (They were not out to cause me stress. They just didn't know better and continued a parenting pattern they learned from their parents.)

Also, traveling, living overseas, and getting to know various people opened my eyes and mind. Suddenly, I realized that most of the things I complained about were within my control, which meant I could change them.

I realized that many of the things that happened to me didn't just 'happen'; they were the results of my own decisions.

I started to look around my social circle. Why did my friends achieve amazing things, and I didn't? I realized that it wasn't because life was hard on me. My friends *chose* to consistently work hard each day and improve their lives. Once I became aware of this, I recognized that I could also achieve the same results, if not more, by doing what they did and putting in the hard work.

As a result of this mindset shift, that I can do anything I set my mind to, I was able to change many aspects of my life for the better. This included my health, dating life, and business.

So **if I can move from *learned helplessness* to *learned optimism*, so can you**!

Studies have shown that learned optimism positively affects a person's psychological and physical well-being.[14,15] It's also seen as effective for handling stress, negative emotions, and pessimism.[16]

Optimists generally achieve more, lead healthier lives, and experience more happiness in life. On the other hand, pessimists are more prone to give up, suffer from sadness, and not enjoy life.

To explain why things are permanent, ubiquitous, or personal, pessimists and optimists have different explanation styles. Let's say you walk up to a lady at a bar and offer her a drink. She declines your offer.

Pessimists believe this is a permanent trend: *I will never get a girlfriend.* Optimists believe that there's no trend here, and it's a one-off situation: *Ah, that didn't work. No sweat. There are plenty of girls out there who'll like me.*

Pessimists: *I'm not interesting.*
Optimists: *She's not interested in me. That's ok. It doesn't mean I'm uninteresting.*

Pessimists will also take this very personally: *I'm ugly. That's why she humiliated me.*
Optimists will not take things personally so easily: *She was probably not in the mood, or I'm just not her type. No harm, no foul.*

When you have a pessimistic explanatory style, you will have your soul crushed. All my friends who were good with women always optimistically explained things.

Optimism is much more helpful than pessimism, but you also need balance. Someone who's too optimistic may become delusional and be unable to see reality.

For example, say you have a business idea and are naively optimistic about it. Even though the business isn't going anywhere, you keep wasting resources on this idea. Nothing has changed after six months of giving it everything you've got. And still, you say, '*Oh, this part of the project is slow, but the business is wonderful!*'

Eventually, you will lose support for your business, so you think, 'W*ell, maybe they were just in a bad mood today.*'

At some point, optimism needs to give way to reality. Being positive doesn't mean you should be blind, and you need to take responsibility whenever necessary. Otherwise, you will not only lose your business but potentially family, friends, and your life savings.

So, by all means, dive into learned optimism. (It's helped me A LOT!) Trying to see things from different perspectives can be very helpful when dealing with anxiety. Just don't swing too far and lose sight of reality.

So, how do you become a more optimistic person? Here are some things you can do to re-train your brain to be more positive.

1. **Engage in optimistic self-talk.** Promote positivity by modeling positive self-talk. Simple reflections about what you enjoyed about your day, what you're grateful for, and what you intend to do to maximize your next day can be a powerful start to cultivating positive thoughts.

   And don't be shy and give yourself credit whenever you deserve it! For example, did you help a friend? Called someone and made their day? Helped someone cross the street or get something at the grocery store they can't reach? Did you smile at someone?

Also, think of the strengths or skills you possess. You know there's GOOD in you, and you just need to tune into them more.

2. **Practice self-empathy.** BE KIND TO YOURSELF. Acknowledge your feelings and realize that you deserve kindness, understanding, and compassion just like everyone else. By becoming empathic with ourselves, we can understand better what we are going through.

3. **Put more emphasis on intention and effort rather than results.** Build optimism by having the right attitude, to begin with. Positive thinkers always prioritize the *process* over the results. It is important to encourage yourself to partake in activities without thinking about the outcome. Be grateful for your efforts to become someone who believes in themselves and never gives up.

   And if something didn't turn out the way you planned, don't be too hard on yourself. Instead of judging your participation in it as a 'failure', commend yourself for trying and then use that situation as a learning experience. Next time you'll know better, so you'll do better.

4. **Think of happier times.** Bad times are never-ending—if you keep thinking about them. Instead, remember past experiences that made you happy. Visualize that situation; remember what you felt then. Next, think of a past event that initially left you feeling sad but eventually overcame them. Now, let this motivate you. Think, '*if I overcame that, I can overcome this too now*'. (See related exercise, **The Happiness Habit**, on page 77).

5. **Change your perspective.** *What else could be true?* If you're a pessimist, you need to constantly challenge your automatic negative way of thinking. Over time, you won't even need to shift your perspective. You'll find that

you've broken the habit of thinking negatively and that thinking positively is now your nature.

6. **TUNE OUT negativity.** Look around you? Is anyone or anything contributing to your negativity? For example, are you at a job you're miserable in? Does the news depress you? Do you have a friend that does nothing but complain? (I mentioned before that it's said we're the average of our five (5) closest friends[5], so make the effort to find those who support and motivate. Don't surround yourself with people who bring you down.)

List these external sources and plan how you can change *your* situation (not them).

As I've previously shared, I realized at one point that my family was the source of my negativity. So as hard as it was to do, living away from them (I moved to another continent!), at least for a while, was one of the best things I've ever done for myself.

WORKBOOK: WEEK 3 – Learned Optimism

Exercise: The ABCDE Model

The **ABCDE Model** was developed by Martin Seligman[13] to gauge your current mindset and to help you become more optimistic.

Adversity: What difficult situation have you experienced recently?

> *Example: I'm on a new diet, and it's frustrating me.*

Belief: What are the thoughts running through your mind about this adversity?

> *Example: I just don't have willpower. I'm never going to reach my goals. It's too hard.*

Consequence: What consequences and behaviors resulted from your beliefs in step 2?

> *Example: The thought that I don't have willpower prevented me from meal planning and prepping. (What's the point?)*

Disputation: Argue or dispute your beliefs in step 2.

> *Example: Willpower... I don't have it, or I'm not using/cultivating it? Maybe I just do this one meal at a time. Then it won't be too hard.*

Energization: How do you feel now that you've challenged your initial (automatic?) beliefs?

> *Example: I feel a bit pumped up again. I'll check out IG and Pinterest and look at some simple healthy recipes for inspiration. I'll make a 3-day meal plan and see how I go about that.*

Now, it's your turn! Please fill out the following.

A Adversity	_____ _____ _____
B Belief	_____ _____ _____
C Consequence	_____ _____ _____
D Disputation	_____ _____ _____
E Energization	_____ _____ _____

IMPORTANT: Please remember that becoming more optimistic in life is an ongoing process. Each time you face a challenge, I encourage you to go through this exercise. Repetition is vital if you want to shift away from one learned mindset to a new one.

You'll find it easier to identify your pessimistic (negative) beliefs and challenge them with continued practice. And in doing so, become more optimistic (positive) about yourself and life.

You've got this!

Exercise: The Happiness Habit

In my journey, I came across a book by *Shawn Achor* called *The Happiness Advantage*[17]. In it is an exercise that has helped me develop the habit of thinking and building happy memories. And in doing so, I was able to adjust my way of thinking from looking at the negative to looking for the positive things in life. I hope this exercise helps you too.

Write down three (3) things that you are grateful for today.

1.)

2.)

3.)

−OR−

Write down one (1) positive event that has happened in the last 24 hours.

NEXT...

Select a positive event from either of your lists above and then do this for 30 consecutive days.

I will _____ for 30 days.

Anxiety and the Wise Mind

Unlike other types of therapy where you're asked to delve into your past, DBT focuses more on the here and now. So, if you're seeing or planning to see a DBT therapist, you'll most likely be asked to respond about current pain points in your life.

The discussion may go into your past and why those pain points developed, but the focus is on how to solve the issues you're currently facing. DBT teaches you to think logically, not emotionally, to respond to problems.

And here's where you learn about the DBT concept called **WISE MIND**.

According to DBT, our minds have two sides: the **EMOTIONAL** and the **REASONABLE** sides. Both sides have their pros and cons, and there is no judgment about which one is better.

The **EMOTIONAL MIND** is when we let our **feelings take control** of our thoughts and actions. Sometimes, people have a sense of self-stigma and wonder why they aren't more 'reasonable'. But being reasonable all the time isn't possible—because we're humans. And humans have emotions.

Further, emotions do not have to be negative. Overly emotional people do get labeled as people who have outbursts but being in your emotional mind could be something as simple as expressing love.

The **REASONABLE MIND** is when **logic takes control**. We weigh the pros and cons and then decide—based on facts—the best way to move forward. For example, you want to fit in a daily exercise routine. There's a gym five minutes away from your office, but you don't like getting caught in rush hour traffic at the end of your day. So, you *reason out* that going to the gym before work is the best solution for you.

DBT states that by combining these two parts of our minds, we create a third mind called the **WISE MIND**. This is taking the best components of our emotional and reasonable minds to arrive at decisions we feel good about, instead of reacting at the moment (knee-jerk reaction) and then having more regret later.

People who suffer from anxiety are prone to let their Emotional Minds rule. However, it's not that you never practice your Wise Mind either. For example, when speaking to your significant other (SO) about what to have for dinner, you're probably using your Wise Mind there.

Your Reasonable Mind is taking stock of the ingredients you have on hand, and you're probably considering what you had yesterday. But because you love your partner, your Emotional Mind is considering what they would want to eat. So, the Wise Mind is the marriage between your emotional and rational minds.

EMOTIONAL MIND   **REASONABLE MIND**

I accept these emotions.
My feelings are valid.

Ruled by emotion,
mood, feelings, urges.

WISE MIND

Ruled facts, reason,
logic.

I just need to stay calm here.
BREATHE.
I don't need to react now.
ZOOM OUT.
Ok, what do I know FOR
SURE?
What's the best solution?

anger
sadness
stress
anxiety
bitterness
fear

experience
information
research
data
logic
facts

Wise Mind Qualities

The Wise Mind is **calm and peaceful**. It honors the Emotional Mind while adding information from the Reasonable Mind.

With the Wise Mind, you are in control of your emotions. Your feelings are valid, and you are NOT judging them. You're not letting them rule you, and you're not letting logic (Reasonable Mind) be your sole guide. You're being guided by your inner wisdom here.

You can feel your emotions, no matter how extreme they may be.
You are also able to access information and knowledge.
Your emotions and your reasoning guide you.

The Wise Mind is **purposeful**. You use your inner resources (emotion and reason) to decide your next steps, knowing that this will produce the best outcome for you.

The Wise Mind is **flexible and open to change**. Although it draws from past experiences, it's not stuck to a routine. It's flexible, open, and willing to the best solution present at the time.

The Wise Mind is **good at conflict resolution**. Rather than being stuck in an all-or-nothing mentality, it can integrate emotional and rational thought and connect with others with compassion.

Please note that **we all have the WISE MIND in us**. It's just that when dealing with anxiety and many other mental health conditions, we tend to lean on our Emotional Mind, which, unfortunately, doesn't give us the best results.

One of the most effective ways to cultivate your Wise Mind is to develop one of the core skills in DBT—**mindfulness**.

The Brain-Altering Power of Mindfulness

Mindfulness is one of the most effective ways to re-train how you think. And no, this is not woo-woo science.

Studies have shown that mindfulness (particularly mindful meditation) can literally change the structure and function of your brain.[18,19,20] This is important for anyone with a mental health condition because mindfulness causes us to be less reactive to unpleasant internal events and more contemplative, which leads to positive psychological results.[21]

Top 5 Ways to Be More Mindful

Mindfulness is being in the moment. It's awareness of what is inside and outside you at any given time. In addition to having a daily meditation habit, the following will also help you cultivate mindfulness.

1. **Focus on your breathing.** One of the ways you can calm the chaos inside and outside you is to pay close attention to your breathing. Close your eyes and breath in for a count of four, hold that breath for a count of four, release your breath for a count of four, stay still for another count of four—and then do it all over again for a total of 5 minutes. This is called Square Breathing or Box Breathing.

   Tip: After you've mastered Square Breathing, you can try the 4-7-8 Breathing exercises on page 87.

2. **Use your five senses.** We don't notice it, but our senses are simultaneously working 24/7. To be more mindful, practice using and focusing on one sense at a time.

   What are you seeing? Take note of a color. Marvel at it, and then close your eyes.
   What are you hearing? Focus your whole attention on that sound.
   What are you smelling? Inhale deeply. What scent is it? What memory is it evoking?
   What are you touching? Reach out and touch something. Is the texture smooth or rough? Hard or soft? Can you trace a pattern?
   What are you tasting? Did you just have coffee? Is it lingering in your taste buds?

   Tip: Try the 5-4-3-2-1 Grounding Technique exercise on page 88.

3. **Break down and understand your emotions.** Often, we get anxious because of a tidal wave of emotions. We get so caught up that we can't distinguish one emotion from the other, so we feel confused and overwhelmed.

So, the next time you feel anxious (or any strong emotion), don't fight it; accept it. That's right, accept the tidal wave.

After that, just be curious and explore your emotions. WHAT exactly are you feeling? WHY are you feeling this way? Remember, you're not your emotions. Your emotions are just an offshoot of something else.

4. **Take multiple 5-minute MINDLESS breaks.** It sounds simple, but when was the last time you took a break and did absolutely nothing? Often, if we ever take a break, we rush to get a cup of coffee and then gulp it down to get back to work. Or we may take a break, but our minds are stuck to what we were doing... thinking, planning, imagining our next steps.

So, this time, take a 5-min break, go somewhere and think and do nothing as best you can.

Tip: Don't know what to do during your break? Do the **Body Scan** exercise on page 89.

5. **Meditate.** Meditation is a form of mindfulness. Many people interchange these words but the simplest description, I believe, is this: *"mindfulness is the awareness of something, while meditation is the awareness of nothing"*[22]. Also, mindfulness is a quality or character you have, while meditation is a practice.

I'm a big believer in meditation as a form of mindfulness. It helps me calm my anxious and hyperactive mind.

I like to schedule 10 minutes to meditate in the morning. This centers me so that I don't get into a frantic state of mind. I then do another 10 minutes of meditation before bed to help me wind down. I find a few apps on the market helpful, such as Simple Habit, Headspace, and Calm. I recommend testing out different apps to see which works best for you.

Top 5 Ways to Make Meditation a Daily Habit

If you're new to meditation or have trouble making it a routine, here are some tips to help you succeed.

1. **Create a consistent schedule.** To build a new habit, you must be consistent in cultivating it. I advise that you practice mindfulness at the start of your day. You can do it in bed after you open your eyes or go to a place in your home where you can have at least 10 minutes of quiet before interacting with anyone. You're making 'waking up' your 'trigger' to meditate this way.

2. **Keep it simple at first.** Don't have any 'goal'. There's nothing specific you need to focus on or think about. Meditation can be as simple as taking a hot cup of your favorite beverage in the morning, going to a quiet place, and then focusing on the sensation of drinking.

   For example, as you sip, take note of the warm steam touching your face, the delicious smell of your dink, the liquid touching your lips, the sensation of swallowing, and feeling that warm liquid go down your throat.

3. **Meditate for as long, or as short, as you like.** There's no exact length of time required for meditation, and it's really more about making it a habit and

engaging in actual meditation. Starting at 5 minutes and slowly working up to 15 minutes is great if you're a beginner.

And don't worry that 15 minutes is too short to make any impact. A 2018 study showed that meditating for just 13 minutes daily for eight consecutive weeks lowered negative moods, improved attention, and working memory, and decreased anxiety.[23]

4. **Forgive yourself repeatedly.** Many people find meditation difficult because it's actually hard to quiet the mind. We're so used to this internal chaos!

However, compassion and forgiveness are crucial when integrating a new self-care practice like meditation, so note the following.

- Forgive yourself when you forget to practice.
- Don't punish yourself for getting caught up in everyday busyness.
- When meditating, forgive yourself if your mind starts to wander incessantly.
- Don't punish yourself when you don't meditate regularly.
- Don't spend too much time contemplating what you didn't do.

5. **Make meditation fun!** Let's face it, sitting, standing, or pacing for x minutes can get boring. So why not spruce up the moment?

For example, treat yourself to some meditation music and play it in the background during your practice. (I personally like nature sounds.) You can also use a guided meditation app (like the ones I mentioned above), find some on YouTube, or buy guided meditation audiotapes. I also really like lighting scented candles with wooden wicks. I close my eyes, listen to the sound of the wooden wick, and imagine a log fire burning.

Mindfulness and meditation are developed through constant practice. And as with any new skill, it helps to start practicing them *when you don't need it.*

You're introducing (or advancing) something new in your life, so practice under easier conditions. This way, you'll be able to adopt them in your life faster, and they'll become 'automatic' when you need them the most.

WORKBOOK: WEEK 4 – Mindfulness

Exercise: 4-7-8 Breathing Technique

This advanced breathing technique will help you slow down your mind, and it will help you bring balance to your mind and body and help reduce stress and anxiety.

Find a comfortable position.

INHALE for 4 counts through your nose.

HOLD YOU BREATH for 7 counts...

EXHALE for 8 counts through your mouth.

Do this for 4 times.

Remember, consistency is important! So please do breathing practice 2x daily for 4 weeks.

5-4-3-2-1

Grounding technique

A calming technique that connects you with the present by exploring the five senses.

Instructions: Sitting or standing, take a deep breath in, and complete the following questions.

5 — 5 things you can see

4 — 4 things you can touch

3 — 3 things you can hear

2 — 2 things you can smell

1 — 1 thing you can taste

Exercise: Mindfulness Body Scan

This mindfulness exercise will help calm your nerves, focus your thoughts, and center your being.

1. Sit or lie down, whatever is most comfortable for you.

2. Close your eyes.

3. Do the Square Breathing exercise (page 59) for 4 cycles.

4. Starting with the top of your head, become aware of your scalp.

5. Notice any areas of tension. Breathe in and as you breathe out... soften and relax that part.

6. Next, become aware of your forehead.

7. Notice any areas of tension. Breathe in and as you breathe out... soften and relax that part.

8. Continue down until you've covered your whole body.

WORKBOOK: WEEK 5 – WISE MIND

Exercise: WISE MIND

The Wise Mind will come naturally to you as you develop mindfulness. This exercise makes use of a Breathing technique to arrive at Wise Mind.

1. Find a comfortable position.
2. Using the Square Breathing technique:
   a. Breathe in while saying the word "Wise" to yourself. Focus all your attention on that word.
   b. Hold your breath.
   c. Exhale while saying the word "Mind" to yourself. Focus all your attention on that word.
3. Continue until you sense that you've successfully arrived at Wise Mind.

WISE MIND

EMOTIONAL
MIND

REASONABLE
MIND

Chapter 4: ADD & ADHD

"For all the hoopla you read and hear about the overdiagnosis of ADD and the overuse of medication-indeed, serious problems in certain places—the more costly problem is the opposite: millions of people, especially adults, have ADD but don't know about it and therefore get no help at all."

- Edward M. Hallowell, M.D.
Delivered from Distraction: Getting the Most out of Life with Attention Deficit Disorder

What is ADHD?

Attention Deficit Hyperactivity Disorder (ADHD) affects millions of adults. According to a 2016 study, 2.8% of adults *worldwide* are affected by this condition.[24]

Despite this, scientists believe that ADHD in adults is usually underdiagnosed since diagnostic criteria were developed primarily for children and because adults with ADHD frequently have concurrent mental problems that may mask ADHD symptoms.

Many attention-related symptoms, such as trouble focusing, hyperactivity, and impulsive conduct, describe ADHD. It's a developmental condition, which means it lasts a lifetime.

Some people have ADHD, but it is inattentive, so they do not exhibit hyperactivity or impulsive behavior. Others are simply hyperactive-impulsive rather than inattentive, though this is less common. Many suffer from both inattention and impulsivity, as well as hyperactivity.

It is critical to highlight a misperception concerning ADHD among those who believe they have it or have been diagnosed with it. Everyone appears to believe they have ADHD, and while many are on the spectrum at some point, if you have occasional inattention that does not affect your functioning and you are not very concerned about it, you probably do not qualify for that diagnosis.

Many people believe they have ADHD when they cannot sit down and read a book for more than an hour or when they are unable to focus during a discussion. ADHD should be distinguished from simply being uninterested in what is happening at the time. Understandably, this can be even more confusing today— thanks to social media

Today's society promotes a lot of inattention. There is a lot of material out there, and there is a lot of research that shows that the more time you spend on social media, the more likely you are to display indicators of ADHD.

Although social media does not cause ADHD, the more you use it, the more inattentive you will become. For example, when you switch on CNN or any other all-news channel, there is a stock ticker at the bottom and a scrolling text bar with all the headlines and a weather ticker. Everything appears to be a breaking story, which is absurd! It's a lot of stimulation for anyone.

Work, school, kids, emails, appointments, projects, deadlines, family, friends— they are all fighting for our attention. And with continuous notifications from our phones, this has gotten much worse.

So, we are all bombarded with information from all angles, but it is different when you have ADHD symptoms.

Due to the emotional dysregulation in adults with ADHD, they find it more difficult to deal with frustration. They're less patient, and their minds may be confused and muddled, making planning and organizing difficult.

Where Things Get Difficult

Depression is the most prevalent co-occurring disorder among people with ADHD. As you might expect, when a child with ADHD performs poorly in school, they develop anxiety and feel bad about themselves. As a result, they start to develop symptoms, such as fidgeting, constantly talking, or interrupting others, which get them into trouble.

Inattentive ADHD, on the other hand, is far more difficult to detect. It manifests as a lack of concentration, simple mistakes, difficulty keeping focus, not listening when spoken to, not following through on directions, and failing to complete assignments.

And because inattentive ADHD is difficult to diagnose, many people never receive a diagnosis or do not receive one until they are far into adulthood.

Anxiety is often secondary to ADHD as it can make people feel inept, leading to performance anxiety, feelings of inadequacy, and clinical anxiety.

Furthermore, a subset of children and adults with ADHD is at a **higher risk of substance abuse and alcoholism.**[25,26]

Finally, individuals with ADHD are at a **higher risk of suicide ideation** since they are predisposed to a variety of psychological issues and dealing with other learning impairments. Due to the complexities and prevalence of mental diseases such as depression among persons with ADHD, this area of inquiry is severely under-researched.

Differentiating ADHD symptoms from learning problems and mental diseases might present several difficulties. A healthcare expert should be consulted to establish an individual's exact needs.

How to Cope with ADHD

People with adult ADHD often dislike schedules, so they may choose to work in more entrepreneurial occupations where they can wake up and start working whenever they want—even if that means working at night. (I began my own business because I wanted to be able to work my own hours.)

However, this situation may aggravate ADHD in some people who need the structure to focus better. It is more difficult to control symptoms when you need to schedule your life around your ADHD and are continually awake and tired due to not sleeping each night properly. As a result, your next day is disrupted, making you less productive and focused.

 By the way, are you enjoying the book so far? If so, please share your thoughts and leave a quick review. Your feedback is appreciated. Thank you!

So, even though you may want to be free with your schedule. It's important to still have structure to cope with ADHD.

For instance, if you're prone to losing your keys or wallet as you walk out the door, you should develop a habit of placing them in your jeans or backpack the night before if that's what you can't leave home without. If you frequently forget tasks, you may want to develop the habit of keeping To-Do lists.

Another way to manage ADHD is to nurture the DBT core skill called Interpersonal Effectiveness.

Interpersonal Effectiveness

Interpersonal Effectiveness refers to skills that foster healthy relationships.

Getting along with others while asserting your needs is essential to maintaining healthy relationships. To achieve this, you need to find that balance between taking care of yourself, your needs, and others.

Interpersonal Effectiveness in DBT means learning these three skills: Objective Effectiveness, Relationship Effectiveness, and Self-Respect Effectiveness.

Objective Effectiveness is about getting what you want out of a situation. The exercise D.E.A.R.M.A.N. on page 97 will help you dissect a situation where you are trying to get something you want, like a resolution with a loved one.

Relationship Effectiveness is also about getting what you want out of a situation with someone you care about, but it also helps you see the other person's perspective. And in doing so, you may come to a compromise. The exercise G.I.V.E on page 99 will help you develop this trait.

Self-Respect Effectiveness keeps your needs, ideals, and morals in balance when facing conflict. In an emotional scenario, it's crucial to remind yourself that you have principles that you want to adhere to, even if someone you care about disagrees with you. This skill allows you to concentrate on facts, which is very useful during emotionally charged situations. The exercise F.A.S.T on page 101 will help you with this.

Exercise: D.E.A.R.M.A.N.

The D.E.A.R.M.A.N. exercise helps you develop the skill of asking for something respectfully and effectively, which builds and maintains relationships, regardless of the outcome of your request.

Describe the situation simply. Stick to the facts. Say exactly what you're reacting to.

Example: You said you would be home for dinner by 7 PM.

Your turn: _____

Express your thoughts or feelings about the situation. Use "I" statements.

Example: I feel taken for granted when you don't tell me you'll be late.

Your turn: _____

Assert your position respectfully but not in an aggressive manner.

Example: I would really like it if you call me when you're going to be late for dinner.

Your turn: _____

Reinforce (reward) when you get what you want or need.

Example: Thank you, babe. I would really feel so much better if you did that.

Your turn: _____

Mindful. Stay focused. Don't worry about the past or the future. Just stay on topic.

> Example: I would like to hear that you understand where I'm coming from.

Your turn: _____

Appear confident. Show confident verbal and non-verbal cues. Do not apologize.

> Example: (Sit or stand up straight. Maintain eye contact. Use a confident tone of voice.) I hope I'm getting across to you because my feelings won't change.

Your turn: _____

Negotiate - If the outcome you want doesn't appear to be within reach, negotiate.

> Example: How about you just text me if you're running late?

Your turn: _____

Exercise: G.I.V.E.

Relationships aren't only about getting what we need. They're also about considering the needs and wants of the other person. The G.I.V.E exercise will help you achieve relationship effectiveness by fostering positive interactions.

Gentle. Approach with gentleness. Don't attack, threaten or express judgment during your interactions. The best communication happens when neither party feels defensive.

What's your request?

Interested. Listen to the other person without interrupting. Expressions of interest can be verbal (e.g., ok, uh-huh, etc.) or non-verbal (e.g., keeping eye contact, not fidgeting or looking at your phone, etc.)

What's YOUR way of showing interest?

Validate. Confirm you hear the other person by echoing their thoughts and emotions back to them. You might say, "*I understand this is frustrating for you too. I'm not happy you feel that way at all.*"

What do you want to say back?

Easy Manner. Throughout the conversation, present yourself as relaxed and comfortable. Act light-hearted and have an easy attitude. (Message to the other person: you're not difficult to deal with.)

How do you convey friendliness to others?

Exercise: F.A.S.T.

Sometimes, in relationships, you might betray your own values and beliefs to receive approval or get what you want. The F.A.S.T. exercise below will help you achieve self-respect effectiveness.

Fair. Be reasonable. Respect your rights and that of others. Avoid being emotional and dramatic outbursts. Stick to the facts.

What's a better way of saying, "You're not hearing me!"

(No) Apologies. Don't apologize for making a request, voicing an opinion, or disagreeing. The only time to apologize is if you've done something wrong.

What's a better way of saying, "I'm sorry I feel this way."

Stick to your values. Stand up for what you believe in. Don't compromise your values just to be liked or to get what you want.

List down 3 things you will not compromise on.
1.)
2.)
3.)

Be Truthful. Be honest and don't lie, exaggerate or act helpless to get what you want.

Think about an incident in the past where you may not have been truthful.
What you said/did….
What you should have said/done…

Chapter 5: Phobias

"Usually, the term phobia refers to the psychological fear of the human mind from something that poses a threat. But when a species starts using the term fear against a biological portion of itself, there is nothing more demeaning than this."

- Abhijit Naskar, The Islamophobic Civilization: Voyage of Acceptance

A phobia is a persistent, uncontrollable fear of a specific object, place, or activity. It's usually characterized by the rapid onset of intense fear, and it usually lasts over six months.

According to the National Institute of Mental Health (NIMH), about 10% of people in the U.S. have specific phobias, 7.1% have social phobias, and 0.9% have agoraphobia.[27]

Where do phobias originate?

Many individuals believe that phobias are a natural part of our evolutionary process as a species. To survive, we needed to be afraid of some things. If our forebears came across anything dangerous, such as a spider or snake, it's understandable that they would be afraid of being bitten, poisoned, or even killed.

So, evolution has given us this built-in readiness to be afraid for our own protection. Still, some phobias may develop due to a negative experience. For instance, being bitten by a dog at a very young age may develop cynophobia (fear of dogs).

However, left untreated, phobias can be harmful. For example, fear of injections (trypanophobia) can prevent an individual from seeking much-needed medical treatment. People afraid of germs (mysophobia) may develop abnormal cleaning behaviors, such as excessive hand washing or acute concern about germs or pathogens, leading to OCD.

Distress Tolerance

One way to manage phobias is to develop *distress tolerance*, one of the core DBT skills.

Distress tolerance skills help people cope with overwhelming negative emotions. With a low threshold for distress, individuals may become overwhelmed even with relatively mild stress, resulting in negative behaviors.

DBT teaches us that pain will occur at times, but the best course is to learn to accept and cope with discomfort.

Distress tolerance requires **Radical Acceptance** as a core component. When a person cannot change the situation, they must experience it and accept it as reality without judgment. Complete acceptance makes us less prone to persistent and intense negative feelings.

Radical Acceptance involves recognizing and accepting the situation AS IS instead of trying to change it. Remember accepting is not the same as liking or condoning something. When you accept the problems you cannot control, you will feel less anxiety, anger, and sadness.

Despite the simplicity of the idea of Radical Acceptance, it can be tricky in practice, particularly when faced with circumstances that we feel are simply completely unfair or unjustified. Still, if you have no power to change these circumstances, then you must accept them AS IS—no matter how painful they may be.

For example, if you experience trauma, it could devastate you. But if you stay in that state of devastation, you cannot move on. In contrast, if you accept the event as is, knowing that there's nothing you can do to change what happened, you can move forward on a healing path.

Dwelling on negative things, even if it is someone else's fault, can be debilitating. As such, you need to constantly work at accepting the situation.

Tip: The exercise **Turning the Mind** (page 106) will help you develop radical acceptance of any situation.

When it comes to my father, I've practiced radical acceptance. My dad is a hoarder, and I have learned to accept him for who he is. I cannot change who he is, but I can change how I react to him and what I can do. I moved out to gain my own mental clarity and space.

It didn't happen overnight. I had to work at it. But in the end, accepting him and the situation is what healed me.

WORKBOOK: Week 7 – Distress Tolerance

Exercise: Turning the Mind

Turning the Mind to acceptance needs constant practice. When we don't get our way, we tend to reject the situation instead of trying to accept it. This exercise is all about trying, over and over and over again, to go in the direction of acceptance.

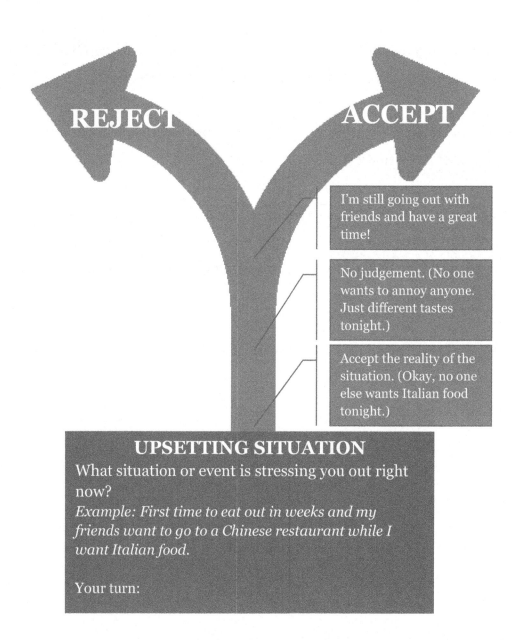

REJECT

ACCEPT

I'm still going out with friends and have a great time!

No judgement. (No one wants to annoy anyone. Just different tastes tonight.)

Accept the reality of the situation. (Okay, no one else wants Italian food tonight.)

UPSETTING SITUATION

What situation or event is stressing you out right now?

Example: First time to eat out in weeks and my friends want to go to a Chinese restaurant while I want Italian food.

Your turn:

Exercise: Radical Acceptance Worksheet

Sometimes you run into a problem that is simply out of your control. It can be easy to think, *'this isn't fair'*, even though that way does not help. Radical acceptance refers to a healthier way of thinking. Instead of focusing on what you want to be different, you will recognize and accept the problem or situation AS IS.

Radical acceptance is not the same as accepting or condoning something. Accepting problems out of your control will lead to less anxiety, anger, and sadness when dealing with them.

SITUATION - Describe a stressful or negative situation.

Example: I wasn't selected for a job I feel I was the best candidate for.

TYPICAL THINKING - Write down your thoughts and feelings.

Example: This isn't fair! I did and said everything right. They can't do this to me.

RADICAL ACCEPTANCE - Write down a statement of acceptance.

Example: This is frustrating, but I ACCEPT they felt someone else would be a good fit.

Self-Soothe with 5 Senses

Find a pleasurable way to engage each of your five senses. Doing so will distract you from what is making you feel anxious. (i.e., Go for a walk somewhere and pay attention to what you see)

Exercise: A.C.C.E.P.T.S.

Negative emotions will usually pass or at least lessen in intensity over time. To help speed up this process, it can help if you can DISTRACT YOURSELF until the emotions subside. This is what the following exercise is all about.

ACTIVITIES: Engage in activities that require thought and concentration.

Example: gardening, baking, exercising, talking to my best friend

Your list:

_____

_____

CONTRIBUTING: Focus on someone other than yourself. Volunteer or do a good deed.

Example: create a care package for someone, call mom

Your list:

_____

_____

COMPARISONS: Look at your situation compared to something worse. Remember a time when you were in (more) pain.

Example: when my father died

Your list:

_____

_____

EMOTIONS: Do something that will create the opposite emotion you feel right now.

Example: swimming, dancing, watching funny YouTube videos

Your list:

_____

_____

PUSHING AWAY: Push negative thoughts out of your mind. Refuse to think about a situation until a better time.

Example: square breathing, watch a romantic-comedy film

Your list:

_____

_____

THOUGHTS: Replace negative, worrying thoughts with activities that keep your mind occupied.

Example: say a prayer, solve a Sudoku puzzle

Your list:

_____

_____

SENSATIONS: Find safe physical sensations to distract you from negative emotions.

Example: Five Senses exercise (page 79)

Your list:

_____

_____

Chapter 6: PTSD & Panic Disorders

"PTSD: It's not the person refusing to let go of the past, but the past refusing to let go of the person. When we feel weak, we drop our heads on the shoulders of others." - Anonymous

Living with PTSD can be a daily battle. A reader, RB, has this to say about her battle with PTSD after childhood trauma.

"For most of my adult life, I have woken up with a sore jaw and tight muscles. This is a direct outcome of the trauma that occurred in the middle of the night.

My mother was a severe alcoholic, and she would become quite volatile with her boyfriend of the week. She would have loud, violent fights with him and whoever was around. If there wasn't anyone to fight with, she would call her brother or mother and fight over the phone.

This would wake us kids often and because I was the oldest, I comforted my younger siblings all through the night. My mother was a functional alcoholic, so she would act like nothing was wrong in the mornings before work and school.

Those tight muscles I deal with every morning are my body's way of protecting myself while I sleep. Years later, I guess it's something my body and brain can't shake. Sometimes I can still hear her yelling and breaking glass in my dreams. I don't know what 'restful sleep' is. I don't think I've ever had them."

What is PTSD?

An individual suffering from Post-Traumatic Stress Disorder (PTSD) shows disturbing behaviors after experiencing a traumatic event, such as a natural disaster, combat, or assault. People with PTSD experience intense fear, helplessness, or terror in response to the event that threatened their safety.

PTSD sufferers avoid reliving the event, avoid any reminder of the situation, and are hypervigilant. There is a general numbing feeling over them, and persistent signs of extreme emotions such as irritability, complete distrust of others, and angry outbursts are present. They also report feeling disconnected from their lives and losing control.

PTSD symptoms normally appear within three months of the stressful event; however, symptoms can appear later. To be diagnosed as a PTSD patient, the symptoms must last for more than one month and be severe enough to interfere with daily life, such as work, relationships with friends and family, behaviour in social gatherings, etc. Symptoms must also be unconnected to medication, substance abuse, or another illness.

PTSD symptoms are wide and varied, so professionals have broken them into four main categories. (PTSD requires at least one or two symptoms from each of these four categories to coincide.)

1. **Intrusion symptoms** include flashbacks of the event that occur at times when you unconsciously wish they did not. This can manifest as nightmares or as unexpected ideas.

2. **Avoidance symptoms** are when you evade anything that reminds you of the trauma. For example, people who have been in serious vehicle accidents may never want to drive again.

3. **Negative thoughts or moods associated with the trauma.** Someone who believes they are not going to live very long, for example, has no idea why they believe this; they simply believe that something bad will happen to them in the future.

4. **Being on edge or hyper-reactive** is when someone is on edge or hyper-reactive. They may experience bouts of rage or have problems sleeping because they need to constantly check locks.

PTSD used to be classified as an anxiety disorder. However, with the new diagnostic and statistical manual published in 2013, PTSD was moved to the category of trauma and stress-related disorders. This is significant because PTSD is now classified as more than anxiety.

Some people feel invalidated by this issue of qualifying trauma. Does this mean their traumatic experience isn't 'bad enough' to be diagnosed as PTSD? This is not the intent of the diagnosis.

Specific incidents are excluded as traumatic experiences for PTSD because not all things you experience have a traumatic effect on the symptoms defined for PTSD. However, that doesn't mean that your trauma doesn't make you depressed, ruin your self-esteem, or lead to anxiety. This simply means that your reaction to the trauma is different from what we see in people with PTSD.

On brain scans, we've seen that people with PTSD have changes in areas of the brain like the amygdala and hippocampus that people without PTSD don't have.

The amygdala, which is responsible for some mating functions, memory and storage purposes, and potential threat assessment, become overstimulated. The opposite happens to the hippocampus, which is responsible for helping store long-term memories and acting as a processor between short-term and long-term memory. The conversion of short-term memory into long-term memory is called memory consolidation.

Cortisol can also be released due to hippocampus damage, resulting in risk factors like obesity, alcohol abuse, and other stress-related conditions.

In response to threats, the part of the brain responsible for triggering a fight-or-flight reaction may respond excessively, sometimes in disproportionate ways to the threat itself. The part of the brain responsible for calming this (over)reaction is not functioning correctly.

Studies show that PTSD makes the brain process and store traumatic memories differently from a normal brain. Because of this, a person with PTSD will experience any number of the following: intrusive memories of the event, nightmares, avoidance behaviors, dissociative flashbacks, an exaggerated startle response, hypervigilance, and may engage in risk-taking behavior.

People with PTSD may also attempt more risky behaviors to test if they can get a positive result from a traumatic situation. Gambling, risky sexual activity, driving, or extreme sports can be outlets for PTSD. If you find yourself partaking in risky behavior after a traumatic event, it's time to take a step back and perhaps consult a professional.

C-PTSD

If PTSD is a condition resulting from a specific trauma, Complex PTSD (C-PTSD) results from *repeated trauma.*

Usually, the trauma starts in childhood and can be physical, emotional, or sexual. Neglect or abuse can also cause C-PTSD because it happens during one of the most vulnerable developmental years. Traumatic experiences shape your personality. It's like you have a fracture. People suffering from this can spend years trying to mend the fracture.

When compared to a person with PTSD who may check locks, have flashbacks, refuse to drive, or jump every time they hear a loud noise, C-PTSD may manifest more behaviorally. It can lead to relationship difficulties, low self-esteem, anger issues, and mood instability.

C-PTSD patients may develop depression or anxiety because of these problems, but at the core of the problem is a fracture that occurs because of a traumatic emotional event that happened during one's formative years. So, the baggage from all that trauma is hardwired. How you respond to the world is influenced by this hardwiring.

A person with PTSD may experience changes in their personality, but not to the same extent as those with C-PTSD. Negative thoughts can linger, not necessarily to depression, but negatively affect your outlook. Other symptoms may be memory problems, being irritable all the time, having much shame, and having problems sleeping.

Trauma-based disorders are often complicated by depression, so how can we treat them? If you have significant depression or anxiety symptoms, you can take medication, but treatment for the underlying trauma requires psychotherapy.

One of the therapies for PTSD and C-PTSD is Eye Movement Desensitization and Reprocessing (EMDR). As part of this therapy, patients are encouraged to talk about the trauma they encountered while moving their eyes in response to stimuli in the room. Crossing the midline of your brain is accomplished by moving your eyes back and forth. As you move from side to side, your brain reprocesses how the event has affected you emotionally. This is a very basic explanation of the therapy.

DBT techniques have also been successfully used for PTSD and C-PTSD patients. [28,29]

As DBT was developed by Marsha M. Linehan, Ph.D., for people who suffer from borderline personality disorder (BPD), it can also be used as a form of trauma-based therapy. (BPD is thought to have its roots in childhood trauma and has many characteristics as PTSD and C-PTSD.)

The DBT approach for trauma-based patients focuses on the DBT skill called Emotion Regulation. This approach is considered helpful because the patient is taught coping skills *before* addressing the trauma(s) that brought on PTSD or C-PTSD. It's an interesting approach because it doesn't re-traumatize the patient. There's no need to re-live anything, only how to cope and get out of state one is feeling.

Emotion Regulation

The goal of Emotion Regulation is to understand our emotions and develop the skills we need to manage them, rather than letting our emotions manage us. The objective is to effectively handle negative emotions AND develop positive emotions simultaneously.

As mentioned throughout this book, negative emotions are not bad and shouldn't be ignored. Negative feelings are a natural part of our lives. We just need to acknowledge and accept them as they are. And in doing so, we reduce our vulnerability to them.

When we reduce our vulnerability to negative emotions, we lower our emotional suffering and increase our ability to experience positive emotions.

When you feel something, you usually exhibit a corresponding behavior. When you're very angry, you might have a fight or argument with someone. When you're feeling extreme sadness, you might withdraw from friends.

During these moments, it will help you take a step back and imagine doing the OPPOSITE of what you would normally do or what you think you will do. Doing this will help you change your emotion. (Related **Opposite Action** exercise on page 121.)

For example, instead of yelling, try talking calmly and politely whenever you are angry. If you withdraw when you're sad, make it a point to visit a friend instead the next time you feel this way.

Also, when facing an overwhelming emotion, make it a habit to look at the facts at the moment to help reduce the intensity of these extreme emotions. (Related **Check the Facts** exercise on page 122.) Are you sure the emotions you're having are based on the realities of the situation?

Lastly, let's not underestimate the mind-body connection when it comes to emotional processing.[30] Simply put, we must take care of our bodies to improve our minds. And in doing so, we're better able to regulate our emotions. (Related **PLEASE** exercise on page 123.)

Changing Your Focus from Negative to Positive

Humans tend to focus more on the negative than the positive. A single criticism is more likely to get our attention than ten compliments!

If you notice yourself focusing on the negative aspects of an experience, try to stop and focus on the positive by focusing on the positive aspects of life daily and acknowledging the things that go right, even if things are not perfect. Don't let small problems ruin the moment.

Adding one or two positive activities won't change your life overnight, but the happiness they generate will add up over time. I recommend taking some time, like 15-20 minutes, and writing down all the activities and things that bring joy to your life.

Write it all down on paper or on your notepad app. Then narrow it down to the Top 3 activities and spend at least 20 minutes each day doing one of these activities. For instance, if your Top 3 activities are jogging, reading, and talking with friends, choose one of these, say jogging, and commit 20 minutes to it each day and take steps to make it happen.

For example, you can write down this goal:
For the next seven days, I'll jog for 20 minutes.

Then go out and do it! After seven days, see how you feel. If you feel better, continue doing it. If you don't, consider switching to one of the other activities and repeating the process. Ideally, your activities should stimulate your mind and body simultaneously for that mind-body connection.

The following are some simple positive activities you can start immediately. Of course, this is not an exhaustive list. It's just to give you some ideas and a starting point.

- Eat a good, leisurely meal.
- See a movie.
- Take a tour of a local attraction.
- Enjoy a picnic.
- Take a walk.
- Enjoy a relaxing night at home.
- Visit with family or friends.
- Take up a new hobby.
- Listen to music.
- Have a dance party.
- Bake something.
- Learn a new language.
- Read a book.
- Spend time with your family.
- Take on a new challenge (with friends!).
- Phone a friend.
- Write a letter (your grandma would love it!).
- Break a sweat!
- Start a gratitude journal.
- Do a craft.
- Enjoy some sunshine.
- Take a break from social media.
- Try some yoga.

WORKBOOK: Week 8 – Emotion Regulation

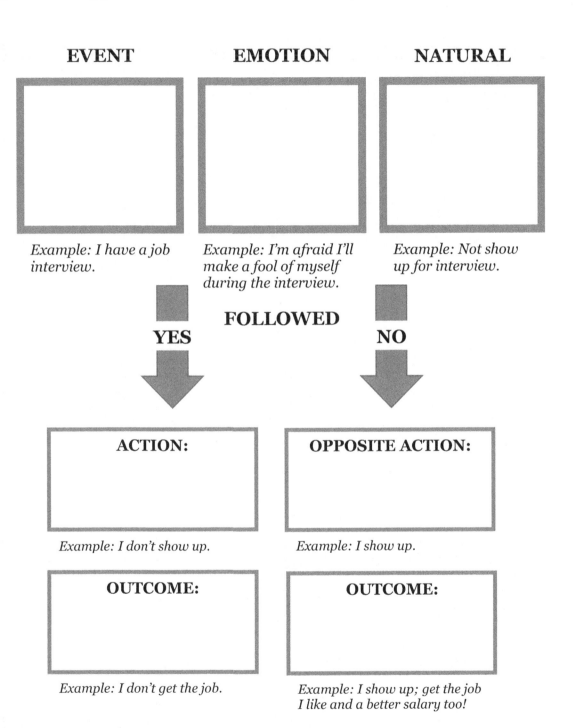

EVENT	**EMOTION**	**NATURAL**
Example: I have a job interview.	Example: I'm afraid I'll make a fool of myself during the interview.	Example: Not show up for interview.

FOLLOWED

YES   **NO**

ACTION:	**OPPOSITE ACTION:**
Example: I don't show up.	Example: I show up.

OUTCOME:	**OUTCOME:**
Example: I don't get the job.	Example: I show up; get the job I like and a better salary too!

Exercise: Check the Facts

Check The Facts

—————— Emotion Regulation Skill ——————

Helping me make sense of a situation where I may have overreacted

Maybe you can look back on your life and think of a few situations where you overreacted. Or you might notice that something once felt like a big deal when it was really unimportant. You can *check the facts* in the moment to reduce the intensity of these extreme emotions. Ask yourself the following questions to check the facts:

What event triggered my emotion?

What interpretations or assumptions am I making about the event?

Does my emotion and its intensity match the *facts* of the situation? Or does it just match my assumptions of the situation?

Exercise: P.L.E.A.S.E.

Your body and mind are closely linked, and the health of one directly affects the other. An unhealthy body will make it difficult to manage your emotions. The acronym P.L.E.A.S.E. can be used to help you remember important aspects of this connection.

Ways I Can Treat **P**hysical Illness (hunger, fatigue)

_____
_____
_____

Ways I can **E**at Healthy

_____
_____
_____

Ways I can **A**void Mood-Altering Drugs (Caffeine, Alcohol)

_____
_____
_____

Ways I Can Make Sure I **S**leep Well

_____
_____
_____

Ways I Can Make Sure I **E**xercise

_____
_____
_____

Chapter 7: OCD & Compulsive Behaviors

"It's like having mental hiccups. Mostly, we can function despite the 'hiccups,' but we're exhausted attempting to carry on as if they didn't exist."

- Sheila Cavanaugh

I've always had some form of OCD, but it didn't become severe until my sophomore year of high school. Before I could leave for school, I had to complete a 'morning ritual'.

As a result, I was frequently late for class, which affected my studies. To avoid having to conduct the morning ritual, I would stay up late at night, generally until 3 or 4 a.m. on weekends, watching TV and eating unhealthy snacks. I was avoiding going to bed so that I didn't have to perform the ritual the next day.

Other common obsessions include seeing blood and being terrified that I will become infected with a disease if I simply see or come into contact with it. This made utilizing a public restroom difficult at times. I would avoid stepping on lines when walking on the sidewalk because it may bring bad luck. In addition, I would tap or check items a specific number of times until the feeling was 'just right', or something horrible would happen.

Fortunately, my OCD was considered relatively minor, and it has substantially improved since then. Other books I've read about treating OCD include *Jeffery M. Schwarz'* book *Brain Lock*[31], which I highly recommend.

In this book, the author treats people with far more severe OCD than I do. One patient, for example, showered for hours, once up to seven hours, because he felt dirty.

Another patient was a man who was so afraid of battery acid that he avoided places where there had been a car accident because he was afraid something would be 'contaminated', and he would go home, change, and throw away his clothes before moving on.

What is OCD?

Obsessive-compulsive disorder (OCD) is characterized by obsessions and compulsions. The Anxiety and Depression Association of America (ADAA) estimates that 2.2. million adults (or 1% of the US population) are affected by OCD.[32]

An obsession is a recurring, persistent, unwelcome, and unnoticed thought, picture, or urge that interferes with interpersonal, social, or vocational functioning. People suffering from OCD believe their thoughts are illogical or excessive, yet they do not believe they have control over them.

Compulsive behaviors or mental acts are things a person repeats to decrease anxiety. Rituals are frequently associated with the obsession, such as repeated handwashing for someone preoccupied with contamination or repeated prayers for someone obsessed with religion.

Following g are some of the most common OCD compulsions.

- Checking rituals, such as checking that the door is locked.
- Counting rituals, such as counting steps or tiles on ceilings.
- Scrubbing and washing until the skin are raw.

- Chanting or praying.
- Touching, rubbing, or tapping (e.g., feeling the texture of the material in a store, touching people, walls, doors, or oneself).
- Hoarding items for fear of throwing away something important.
- Organizing (e.g., arranging and rearranging items on a desk, shelf, or furniture in perfect order; vacuuming the carpet in one direction).
- Rigid performance such as getting dressed in a specific pattern.
- Aggressive urges (i.e., a desire to throw things or hit things).

When an individual's thoughts, ideas, and impulses consume them to the point that they interfere with their life or well-being, they are diagnosed with OCD.

These routines are irrational and strange to OCD sufferers, but they feel forced to perform them to relieve anxiety or prevent awful thoughts. Obsessions and compulsions can cause tremendous misery and embarrassment for those who suffer from them, and they may go to great measures to conceal them.

OCD Causes

Genetics: People with close relatives who got OCD as teenagers (mom, dad, siblings) are more likely to develop OCD. Several genes involved in serotonin transport or response have been connected to the development of OCD. Defects in other genes involved in brain transmission may also contribute to the illness. OCD does not occur in all people who have the linked variants, and some of the variants do not result in OCD.

Brain Structure: Based on differences in the frontal cortex between OCD and non-OCD test subjects, researchers are beginning to pinpoint brain areas that may be affected by OCD. Whether the illness involves alterations in chemical messengers (neurotransmitters) such as serotonin and dopamine is being investigated. A problem controlling the activity and interaction of different brain areas is also thought to contribute to the illness.

A person suffering from OCD finds it difficult to pay attention to events that do not immediately influence them. As a result, they do not automatically retain the events the way we do.

For example, my brain may recognize that I had done something similar, such as locking the front door in the morning. This is known as *implicit learning*. Despite not being actively or expressly focused on shutting the door, I had the impression that I had done so despite having no recollection of it. However, those with OCD may have this difficulty; thus, they may stare at a light switch for a long time and still feel that the switch is off.

People with OCD frequently can't be sure they did something inappropriate because they can't recall *not* doing it. For example, they may be afraid of unintentionally having sex with someone they just met at the bar. Later, they explore their memory for evidence to be absolutely positive that they hadn't molested or abused someone. Unable to find it, they become increasingly terrified and decide that they must have molested someone because they cannot recall not having done so.

Brain imaging evidence suggests that when patients have intrusive obsessions, specific brain areas become more active. These areas are linked to the limbic system, which is thought to be where intense emotions are created. This is why people obsess over things that put them at risk, harm, or shame.

OCD symptoms appear when the limbic system and the prefrontal cortex are dysfunctional. As a result of both of these disorders coexisting, we place an undue emphasis on our thoughts.

When you have episodic memory, you can relive prior experiences in your mind. While I don't recall whether or not I locked the door to my house this morning, this anxiety isn't as important to me as it would be to someone with OCD, who can be extremely anxious about their safety and fearful of making a mistake and being blamed.

Some patients describe their bad thoughts as vivid visuals. When people are terrified, they can sometimes "see" what happens.

If they check their memory repeatedly, they may lose their memory of what they did and did not do, as it becomes more difficult to distinguish between episodes.

Environment: Aside from genetic considerations, researchers investigate environmental factors connected with OCD, such as pregnancy problems and stressful life experiences. A conclusive link between any of them and this condition has yet to be established. An individual's chance of getting OCD may be determined by genetic and environmental variables.

All of these factors appear to impact the existence of OCD, though more research is needed. In all likelihood, one's OCD is caused by a parent who suffers from OCD and grew up in a strict environment where everything had to be neat and done precisely.

OCD Misconceptions

People easily quip, *'I'm so OCD'*, while discussing their eccentric cleanliness, yet these sentiments are quite disrespectful to people who suffer from OCD. Many varieties of OCD have been depicted in popular culture as oddities rather than serious disorders, including characters based on stereotypical OCD features and entire TV shows that exploit people suffering from hoarding behaviors. Many individuals are unaware of how incapacitating this can be.

Furthermore, the caricature of an OCD patient as an extreme "neat freak" fails to convey that, as we've already demonstrated, the condition can emerge in various ways.

Hopefully, knowing these facts can help you understand that this disorder is more than just a quirky personality attribute.

If you have a drug use disorder and one or more of the numerous varieties of OCD, a dual diagnosis treatment program can help you recover.

In a Dual Diagnosis Disorder Inpatient Unit or Outpatient Clinic, professionals will treat both the OCD and the underlying depression that many people suffer from. They also address your substance use medically and provide therapy, education, and support to help you stay away from drugs and alcohol while focusing on your treatment plan for the things that make you who you are.

OCD Categories

According to specialists, OCD types fall into six different categories.

1. Organization

This is possibly the most well-known variety of OCD, and it involves obsessions with objects being in exactly the right spot or being symmetrical. For example, someone may feel compelled to keep all wall hangings level, all labels on pantry cans facing outward, or everything on their workstation totally clean. If the person does not meet the compulsions to have things just so, they may experience unhappiness or fear that the lack of organization will cause them or their loved ones harm

2. Contamination

Those suffering from an obsession or compulsion related to contamination will typically find themselves or their surroundings being washed to a dangerous extent. For example, they may purchase a large quantity of individually wrapped hand soaps, open each packet once, then buy a new one every time they wash their hands.

People with such behaviors tend to be extremely fearful of being infected by bacteria on surfaces. Therefore, those who suffer from this OCD type may go to great lengths to avoid:

- Contact with others.
- Public washrooms.
- Restaurants.
- Handles and doorknobs.
- Medical facilities.
- Enjoying the outdoors.

Mental Contamination

Mental Contamination is much the same as physical contamination, except instead of germs in the physical world, it is internal uncleanliness that is the source of the individual's obsession.

Uncleanliness is often caused by psychological trauma. The sufferer may spend hours and hours washing their bodies if, for example, they are ridiculed or emotionally traumatized by someone. So, a fear of physical illness does not cause compulsions, but emotional damage does.

3. Checking

Checking is an obsession in which a person is preoccupied with the possibility of causing damage or injury by being careless. They may need to double-check something or even look at it for a while before feeling more comfortable. Compulsions might include checking any of the following:

- Window and door locks.
- Water faucets.
- Appliances.
- Wallets.
- Pockets.
- Lights.
- Electrical plugs and sockets.

A checking compulsion might also be manifested in the following conditions.

- Frequently seeking reassurance from friends and/or family members that they're not offended by something the OCD sufferer said.
- Constantly researching symptoms of a disease.
- Concentrating on details to ensure they don't forget anything
- Obsessively reviewing documents before submitting them to ensure nothing offensive has been inadvertently inserted.

4. Hoarding

Hoarding is characterized by:

- Trouble getting rid of old, unusable items.
- A tendency to collect too many useless things.
- Difficulty finding time to organize hoarded objects.

Hoarders will usually have cluttered homes with old and useless items, so they are typically unable to use more than a few square feet of space.

A person with hoarding tendencies may have difficulty disposing of discarded newspapers, plastic bags, and even decayed food.

For several reasons, it is arguably the most dangerous type of OCD. One major threat of an unclean environment is the potential for contracting several illnesses, some of which are deadly.

Hoarders' homes may also be challenging to navigate for reasons other than hygienic ones. The accumulation of materials in hoarders' homes may contribute to a risk for falls, become a fire hazard, and/or prevent the individual from getting out of a burning house in the event of a fire.

Hoarding Types

Following are the three different hoarding types:

1. **Sentimental Hoarding** is when a hoarder attaches a great deal of significance to each item they keep, making it difficult to get rid of it. They may begin to believe that it might be impossible to keep the memory associated with the object if they discard it.

2. **Deprivation Hoarding** is when a hoarder cannot throw away items because they anticipate the possibility that they will need them someday. One example of deprivation hoarding is to wear only one pair of shoes but own fifteen others—just in case.

3. **Preventing Harm to Others Hoarding** is when an individual holds on to broken glass or even human waste that might harm others. Although

these types of fears are irrational, their motive is to protect other people at the risk of their own safety.

5. Ruminations

Rumination is a series of prolonged thoughts on an entirely unproductive topic.

Different from intrusive thoughts, ruminations aren't really objectionable. Some examples are thoughts such as fears of harming someone, religious preoccupations, or intense thoughts of perfection. Instead of suppressing these thoughts, these OCD sufferers may spend hours upon hours every day indulging in them.

6. Intrusive Thoughts

An individual suffering from intrusive thoughts is usually disturbed by them; unlike someone suffering from ruminations

Intrusive thoughts are usually distressing or disgusting ideas that enter people's heads seemingly at random. These obsessions can include hurting a loved one, inflicting harm to a stranger, or even believing that simply thinking about something increases the likelihood of it happening.

A person may need to perform an action to silence intrusive thoughts, such as speaking something aloud or mentally repeating something. People who have intrusive obsessions may have aggressive or dangerous thoughts, but they do not agree with or act on them. In fact, these notions are so diametrically opposed to how people feel that often, they're bothered why their minds even generated the thoughts in the first place.

DBT and OCD

Research has shown that DBT is a viable treatment for OCD.[33,34,35]

The DBT skill **Mindfulness** focuses on being present in the moment, which can help when trying to interrupt or redirect repetitive thoughts and actions.

As an OCD sufferer, thoughts would come back stronger the more I tried to ignore them. By applying the DBT principle of Radical Acceptance, I let my thoughts pass through my mind without judgment, as if I were an observer. I say to myself, "*The OCD is passing through*".

Before DBT, I would get very worried and anxious. I used to entertain every thought, including ideas of self-harm. Now, I have the tools to NOT act upon an intrusive thought just because it comes to me.

Instead of giving in to the compulsion, I engage in other activities. A busy and active lifestyle helps me a lot. I've noticed that my OCD gets worse when I become aware of it or when I'm stressed or anxious. To keep my mind focused and engaged, I work out, do yoga, walk, meditate, etc. Additionally, I feel less stressed and have more energy when I sleep well, eat well, and exercise.

One of the best tips I took away was to be aware of my obsessions and compulsions. Taking note of when I'm obsessed versus when I want to compel myself is important for me to differentiate. *Brain Lock*[31] suggests diverting attention from OCD thoughts by focusing on another task for 15 seconds to a minute.

For example, if I needed to check if the tap was turned off, I would simply take a deep breath, regroup, and walk away. I've also reduced my checking OCD by training myself to check things only once. For instance, if I feel I must check if I locked the door, I would carefully and slowly (mindfully) check that door is locked ONCE and then move on. This is very different from how I was before when I had to check it 10-15 times—and I'd still feel compelled to check it again to be sure.

Once I started to radically accept that I had OCD, I could free myself from the notion that something was wrong with me, and it gave me hope and made my OCD a lot more manageable. Now, I just say, *"It's not me; it's the OCD."*

The DBT skill **Interpersonal Effectiveness** also helped me a lot. Part of my Checking OCD was to constantly seek external reassurance. I was always asking people around me if I offended them. It's very tiring to keep on explaining yourself, but I couldn't help it!

At the same time, I was suffering alone. I was confused and embarrassed about my condition that I didn't communicate my problems to others. No one knew how I was feeling inside. As a result, just like many other OCD sufferers, I isolated myself, and my life revolved around my rituals, which worsened my condition.

Thanks to the DBT interpersonal effectiveness skills I learned, I was able to slowly build positive relationships in my life.

The DBT skill **Distress Tolerance** was instrumental to my healing too. As you've probably deduced by now, my OCD focuses on Organization, Contamination, and Checking. Whenever these would kick in, I would self-soothe (page **Error! Bookmark not defined.**), distract myself (page 110), or do both to get myself out of that situation or way of thinking.

Finally, the DBT skill **Emotion Regulation** assisted me in coping with my obsessions by teaching me how to comprehend my emotions. By understanding the emotions I had while my OCD was kicking in, I managed them to a point where I lessened my emotional suffering.

For example, I was always under great emotional stress and suffering whenever I could not perform my morning ritual before school. If I didn't do them, I would be sweating bullets all day for fear that something bad would happen, which would worsen my anxiety disorder.

The exercise Check the Facts (page 122), in particular, helped me a lot. Whenever I was in fear because I didn't do my routine, this exercise helped me see that my emotions DID NOT fit the facts of the situation. With constant practice, I was eventually able to drastically lessen my feelings of fear because my mind could list down the facts or truths of the situation.

The Importance of Stress Management

OCD is a challenging condition to manage. Trust me, I know. This problem is also readily aggravated when you are under a lot of stress, so in addition to the DBT skills I've adopted, I've also taken active steps to lessen potential stressors in your life. Following are my tips on how you can do this.

1. **Communicate with family and friends and ask for their help.** You need to be honest and open with your loved ones about your OCD. I know it's not easy, but you need to tell them about your situation and ask them to be kind and patient with you.

    Remember, these are the people you surround yourself with, so they have a big impact on how stressful, or not, your life can be. And with their love and support, you'll be much able to cope with your OCD.

2. **Practice gratitude.** Learning to be more grateful has helped me better control my emotions with this condition. When I realized how much worse some people's OCD was than mine, I appreciated what I had.

    Although I wish I didn't have this condition, I am grateful to have excellent health, a home over my head, and the opportunity to grow up in a first-world country. Within human history and among people growing up in true poverty or war, I am within the top 5% of fortunate people. So I know I have a lot to be thankful for.

This is not to deny that OCD is a crippling disorder, but knowing that it can be treated, managed, and improved helped me work on myself to achieve a better life.

3. **Declutter your space.** Another benefitting my emotions and mental health is decluttering my space. I knew I didn't want to wind up a hoarder like my dad, so I set a goal of owning as few things as possible.

When I relocated from Korea to HK for graduate school, I tossed away many items, including clothes that I had only worn a couple of times. So many possessions just added to the stress of moving!

I've steadily reduced my belongings over the years to maintain my environment nice, orderly, and uncluttered. And I've since realized that decluttering my physical space improved my mental space.

4. **Create a 'stress list'.** You may not realize it, but there might be certain people or situations that are guaranteed to stress you out. For example, seeing a particular sibling, extra work tasks on Fridays, a person who has a habit of crossing your boundaries, and so on might be your 'stressors' and exacerbate your OCD. By creating such a list, you can prepare yourself better on how to address them.

For instance, if 'extra work tasks on Fridays' is your stressor, prepare by either ensuring you leave work earlier on Fridays or having a ready list of sentences you can use to say no to the extra workload.

5. **TAKE CARE OF YOUR BODY.** One of the most important things I've learned during my OCD journey is that what I do with my body matters.

For example, I make sure I get **consistent, good-quality sleep**. (According to the National Sleep Foundation, that's at least seven hours.[36]) Sleep affects cortisol, the stress hormone, so I do my best to get at least seven hours of shut-eye by ensuring I stop work at a certain time, stop checking my digital devices at a certain time, go to bed a certain time, and wake up a certain time.

Another thing I do is **get active**. I have a consistent yoga, meditation, and workout routine. All these lower my adrenaline and cortisol levels and increase my body's release of endorphins, the mood-elevating hormone.

I also **eat REAL FOOD** now. One of the ways I dealt with my OCD was to eat unhealthy snacks. For years, I didn't realize that all those chemicals were stressing my body and potentially making my OCD worse!

For example, a 2009 study published in the British Journal of Psychiatry indicated that processed foods may support the development of mental health problems.[37] Research has also shown that people who eat a 'Western diet' (i.e., high on sugar) are 35% more likely to develop depression.[38]

So, I'm more vigilant with what I eat and make sure I only eat food that truly nourishes my body.

WEEK 9 – Mindfulness

To recap, please go back to the **Mindfulness** exercises on page 87. On this page is another exercise to help you cultivate mindfulness in your life: **The Spiral Staircase**.

1. Find a comfortable position. Stand up, sit down or lie down.

2. Imagine a spiral staircase within you.

3. Now, starting at the top, slowly descend the staircase, going deeper and deeper within yourself with each step.

4. Take note of what you're feeling with each step.

5. There is no rush. Do not push yourself any further than you want to go.

6. Take note of the silence.

7. Concentrate your attention on the center of your being as you reach it.

To recap, please go back to the **Interpersonal Effectiveness** exercises on page 97.

One of the important Interpersonal Effectiveness skills to develop is **Objective Effectiveness**, which is **your ability to ask and get what you want from others or in any given situation**.

Often, we get in our own way and don't dare to ask for what we want because of certain 'myths' or ideas in our heads. For example, you don't want to go against your friends because you think they won't like you anymore if you say 'no'. This is a myth. True friends will still like you even if you say 'no' to them every now and then.

So the following exercise is called **Challenging Myths**. For each myth, write a challenging statement that makes sense to you.

Example:
Myth: I don't deserve to have what I want or require.
Challenge:
Everyone deserves to be happy. I deserve to be happy. And to be happy means, I get my way or get to do what I want to do.

Your Turn...
Myth: I don't deserve to have what I want or require.
Challenge:

_____

_____

Myth: If I ask for something, I'm a needy person.

Challenge:

_____

_____

Myth: Before I make a request, I need to know whether or not the person will say yes.

Challenge:

_____

_____

Myth: People will get angry with me if I say 'no'.

Challenge:

_____

_____

Myth: If someone tells me 'no', they don't like me.

Challenge:

_____

_____

Myth: Asking for something is selfish.

Challenge:

_____

_____

Myth: If I can't solve something or need help, I must be incompetent.

Challenge:

_____

_____

Myth: It's not important if I don't have what I want or need; I don't really care.

Challenge:

_____

_____

Myth: No one cares about what I want or need.

Challenge:

_____

_____

To recap, please go back to the Distress Tolerance exercises on page 106. Another exercise to help you when overcome with extreme emotions is this: **TIPP**.

Temperature: Calm down by subjecting your face to cold temperature. You can run the tap and splash your face with cold water, stick your head for a few seconds in the fridge, or simply step outside during cold weather.

Intense Exercise: Calm down your body by engaging in strenuous exercise. Sometimes, just a quick 7-minute routine will do. If not, just go on until you feel your emotions subsiding.

Paced Breathing: Thoughts and emotions racing? Slow down by breathing in slowly, and then exhaling even slower (e.g., breathe in for 4 seconds, exhale for 5 seconds).

Paired Muscle Relaxation: Do this at the same time you do Paced Breathing above. As you breathe in, slowly tense your body muscles (not to the point of cramping!), and then as you breathe out, release all that muscle tension and say to yourself, 'RELAX'.

WEEK 12 – Emotion Regulation

To recap, please go back to the Emotion Regulation exercises on page 121.

One of the ways to cultivate your Emotion Regulation skills is to reduce your vulnerability to negative feelings by increasing your arsenal of positive feelings. The following exercise is called **Building Positive Emotions**, and it will help you define what makes you positive and happy and encourage you to do them more often.

Build Positive Experiences <u>NOW</u>
List 10 things that make you happy. It can be *any* event such as riding your bicycle, taking care of your plants, singing, etc.

    1.)

    2.)

    3.)

    4.)

    5.)

    6.)

    7.)

    8.)

    9.)

    10.)

Select one (ANY one) from the above list and then commit to doing it each day. It doesn't matter what you choose and how long you want to do it. The goal is to do it EVERY SINGLE DAY.

Example:

I choose: yoga

I will practice yoga every day for 30 minutes in the morning.

Your turn:

I choose: _____

I will _____ every day for _____.

Be Mindful of Positive Experiences

Whenever you do the event you chose above, give it your FULL ATTENTION. No multi-tasking, and don't do anything else. In fact, if possible, STOP what you're doing and just absorb the moment. Just experience the positive event.

Today, I felt happy when I:

(Example: Spent time in the kitchen cooking my favorite childhood dish.)

_____

_____

_____

_____

These are the words that describe that event for me:

(Example: relaxed, grateful, in the zone, happy, nostalgic, carefree)

_____

_____

_____

_____

_____

Chapter 8: Supplements and Medications

Disclaimer

Medication and supplements, like any other illness, can have a role. I am not a doctor, and the material in this chapter is based only on anecdotal evidence. Although vitamins and medication can assist, remember that eating a well-balanced, whole-food diet is also crucial for keeping your body and mind healthy and having enough fuel for the day.

Before beginning any supplements or medications on your own, please see your doctor or healthcare expert.

Supplements

Supplements that Help with Anxiety

GABA: Gamma-aminobutyric acid is a neurotransmitter in the central nervous system that operates as an amino acid in the body. GABA inhibits nerve transmission, suppressing neural activity and providing a soothing effect.

Low GABA levels in your body increase the symptoms of persistent anxiety disorders, post-traumatic stress disorder (PTSD), and depression. A lack of GABA activity has been linked to more severe symptoms, whereas a sufficient level of GABA may help calm symptoms and make them more bearable for you.

Melatonin is a sleep aid, and it should not be used on a long-term basis but just when your anxiety keeps you awake. In addition to its antidepressant properties, melatonin may also be used to treat anxiety, sleep difficulties, and circadian rhythm issues.

Melatonin is used as a first-line treatment for patients suffering from insomnia, parasomnia, or irregular circadian rhythms.

Magnesium is a mineral that helps relax muscles and is best taken at night. Due to soil depletion around the world, most individuals are magnesium deficient.

Magnesium may help lower anxiety and tension in the brain. The hypothalamus, a brain region that regulates pituitary and adrenal gland function, is considered to be affected, and these glands regulate your stress response. Leafy greens, nuts, seeds, dark chocolate, avocados, tofu, salmon, dry beans, whole grains, wheat germ, and wheat and oat bran are all high in magnesium.

Men should get 400-420 mg of magnesium each day. Adult women should take 310-320 mg of magnesium per day. (Note: Reduce your dose if you develop diarrhea.)

5-HTP: 5-Hydroxytryptophan is an amino acid that your body naturally produces. 5-HTP supplements are thought to treat depression by increasing serotonin levels. (Note: Do not use an SSRI/SNRI, or you can run into a condition called serotonin syndrome, which can be dangerous.)

Vitamin D, also known as the sunshine vitamin, helps with depression and anxiety. Vitamin D is vital for mood regulation and preventing depression. People suffering from depression who took vitamin D supplements reported an improvement in their symptoms.[39]

Vitamin D is best absorbed by basking in the sun for 20-30 minutes per day. If it isn't an option, supplements will suffice. Adults should consume 600–800 IU per day.

Vitamin C can also enhance your mood by lowering cortisol, a stress hormone created by your body when you are stressed. Vitamin C is also a powerful brain booster! Several studies have suggested that vitamin C may aid in the treatment of oxidative stress-related cognitive disorders such as anxiety.[40] Citrus fruits and vegetables are the best sources of vitamin C. If your diet is low in these foods, a supplement can help. Adults should consume 65-90 mg per day and not exceed 2000 mg per day.

B Complex boosts energy and enhances mood. It also improves your capacity to concentrate and recall information. There is some evidence that multivitamins can help with anxiety symptoms.

According to one study, young adults who took a multivitamin including B vitamins, vitamin C, calcium, magnesium, and zinc for 30 days experienced significantly fewer anxiety symptoms than those who took a placebo.[41]

Furthermore, a meta-analysis of eight trials discovered that taking a multivitamin and multi-mineral supplements for at least 28 days reduced perceived stress and anxiety in healthy individuals.[42] Moreover, high-dose B vitamin supplementation may be more advantageous than low-dose B vitamin supplementation.

Omega 3 fatty acids, particularly DHA, have been related to a lower incidence of depression. DHA aids in creating serotonin, which is crucial for mood regulation. Because omega-3 fats have potent anti-inflammatory qualities, they may aid people who suffer from anxiety. Omega 3 fatty acids can be found in fish and seafood and nuts and seeds.

An analysis of 19 studies found that omega-3 fatty acid treatment reduced anxiety symptoms significantly compared to controls. Over 2,000 milligrams of omega-3s per day were proven to have considerable anti-anxiety effects.[43]

CBD (cannabinoid) is a non-hallucinogenic component of marijuana that has soothing properties. It is not legal everywhere in the world. CBD may also benefit persons suffering from other types of anxiety, such as social anxiety disorder (SAD) and post-traumatic stress disorder (PTSD). It can also be used to treat anxiety-related insomnia.

CBD was researched for its impact on those suffering from depression in 2011. They were given either 400 milligrams (mg) of CBD or a placebo. The CBD consumers reported a drop in their anxiety levels overall.

CBD has also been demonstrated in multiple studies to reduce PTSD symptoms such as nightmares.

Medications

Medications Used for Anxiety, Stress, and Worry

Anti-depressants: It's widely known that depression and anxiety often go hand in hand. There are two kinds of anti-depressants: **SSRIs** and **SNRIs**. Both of these classes take approximately three weeks to start working, and often patients must try different brands and doses of these drugs before settling on one that works for them. Some of these drugs have significant side effects such as headaches, weight gain, and irritability.

Working with your doctor to choose the right medication for you can be a long and frustrating process. Lastly, it's important to remember that medications alone will not fix your anxiety.

SSRI (Selective Serotonin Reuptake Inhibitors) acts on the chemical serotonin to regulate mood and emotion. SSRIs are anti-depressants.

Examples of SSRIs are:
- Citalopram (Celexa)
- Escitalopram (Lexapro)
- Fluoxetine (Prozac)
- Paroxetine (Paxil)
- Sertraline (Zoloft)
- Vortioxetine (Trintellix)

SNRI (Serotonin and Norepinephrine Reuptake Inhibitors) act on the brain chemicals serotonin and norepinephrine to regulate anxiety, mood, and emotion. SNRIs are anti-depressants, but they are also anti-anxiety medications. Additionally, they have been used for chronic pain.

Examples of SNRI are:
- Desvenlafaxine (Pristiq)
- Duloxetine (Cymbalta)
- Levomilnacipran (Fetzima)
- Venlafaxine (Effexor XR)

Anti-anxiety medications are used for people prone to anxiety attacks or panic attacks. Some of the medications used are for when a person is in an acute state of panic or is about to embark on something that may induce a panic attack, such as during a flight or when public speaking).

Examples of Anti-Anxiety Medications are:
- Benzodiazepines (Ativan, Valium, Klonopin, Xanax)

- Buspirone (Buspar)

Medications Used for ADD & ADHD

Stimulants

This drug class has been used to treat ADHD for years, and these drugs work in most cases of ADD/ADHD. Examples of short-acting stimulants include Adderall, Ritalin, Dexedrine, and Focalin. Long-acting stimulants last longer and are more often used. Some of these include Methylphenidate, Adderall XR, and Vyvanse.

Non-Stimulants

Sometimes stimulants do not work for ADHD or cause unpleasant side effects. This class of drugs can help with impulse control, focus, and concentration. Examples of these drugs include Clonidine, Guanfacine, and Viloxazine.

Anti-Depressants

As described above, anti-depressants can help with depression and anxiety, common among people with ADD and ADHD.

Medications Used for Phobias

Medications used for phobias are not usually part of initial treatments. Phobias are treated mainly with therapy; however, medications may be introduced in severe cases.

When medications are introduced for phobias, they will be an anti-depressant. Most SSRIs are excellent for the treatment of social phobias.

MAO inhibitors are sometimes introduced but require careful monitoring due to interactions with other drugs.

Beta-blockers may occasionally be used to block the stimulating effects of adrenaline: increased heart rate and blood pressure, and shaking caused by anxiety.

Occasionally doctors will do short-term therapy using sedative-hypnotic drugs such as Xanax or Valium. These drugs can be habit-forming, so it's best to use them sparingly, if at all.

Medications Used for PTSD & Panic Disorders

Like the other disorders listed, PTSD and Panic Disorders are often treated with anti-depressants, anti-anxiety meds, beta-blockers, and MAOIs, as described above.

Another medication doctors use to help with nightmares or flashbacks is Prazosin (Minipress). This can help your brain "shut off" at night and assist with insomnia and nightmares. Often this med requires dose changes, so it's important to keep a sleep journal and share your findings with your doctor.

In conjunction with these treatments, sometimes antipsychotics are used. Despite the negative connotation of the class name, these meds can help treat PTSD. Examples include Olanzapine, Quetiapine, and Risperidone.

Medications Used for OCD & Compulsive Behaviors

Anti-depressants are the most common drugs that doctors will start with when treating OCD and Compulsive Behaviors. People with OCD will often suffer from depression, so having an SSRI on board can help with both OCD and depression. Specifically, the following medications have been known to work well for people with OCD:

- Clomipramine (Anafranil)
- Fluoxetine (Prozac)
- Paroxetine (Paxil)
- Venlafaxine (Effexor)
- Fluvoxamine (Luvox)
- Sertraline (Zoloft)
- Citalopram (Celexa)
- Escitalopram (Lexapro)

As I have explained, medications are not a one-stop solution, and therapy is one of your best defenses to combat the symptoms associated with these anxiety disorders.

If you need support beyond CBT, DBT, supplements, and medications, the following are a few options to explore with your doctor.

Clinical trials: Test unproven therapies by joining research trials.

Deep-Brain Stimulation: Involves surgical implants of electrodes in the brain.

ECT (ElectroConvulsive Therapy): Involves receiving electric shocks from electrodes attached to your head to induce seizures, which cause your brain to release hormones like serotonin.

While medication helps in some cases, it is not a standalone solution to managing life with an anxiety disorder. I've found using anxiety management techniques, particularly DBT practices, to cope with life's stressors essential to improving my quality of life.

Again, this chapter is not meant to be a medical treatment manual, and everything is based on anecdotal evidence. Before starting any therapy, supplements, medications, or alternative remedies on your own, please speak with your doctor or healthcare professional first.

And if ever you feel you need immediate help, you should contact your local suicide hotline, call 911 if needed, or visit your local emergency department.

Conclusion

There are always ways to improve your situation, regardless of the sort of anxiety you are experiencing or the intensity of your condition. In this book, we discussed a variety of therapies and approaches for improving your thoughts and habits.

Learning to understand what triggers your anxiety, letting go of what no longer serves you, and leaning on resources are all foundations to reducing your anxiety and the symptoms that come with it.

Too frequently, we tend to view worry as something to be avoided at all costs. The truth is that a little anxiety protects us against things that can damage us, and we need it to survive. Plus, there's positive anxiety, such as falling in love, the start of college, our first jobs, our wedding day, and so on!

Managing anxiety and stress is critical to staying healthy, and we must take a step back to realize when worry is normal and when it is stress that must be addressed.

People suffering from anxiety disorders should realize that the goal is efficient stress management rather than complete removal.

You will be better prepared to deal with stress if you take the following steps.

- Consume nutritious foods.
- Get enough sleep and rest.
- Exercise.
- Consume caffeine and alcohol in moderation.
- Set attainable goals and expectations.
- Learn to relax, whatever that means for you.

- And, of course, learn the DBT skills of <u>Mindfulness</u>, <u>Interpersonal Effectiveness</u>, <u>Distress Tolerance</u>, and <u>Emotion Regulation</u> we covered in this book.

You've put a lot of effort into reading this book. Some of it may have been more difficult than you anticipated. But know that all of these will work to help you.

Managing anxiety, or any mental health condition, is a lifelong challenge. So, please do continue to practice the DBT skills you learned here. Don't just go and re-read the chapters and perform the exercises whenever anxiety hits you. You need to make an effort to practice these DBT skills daily so that they become natural to you.

Taking care of yourself is not a linear process. Sometimes, you will come across problems that might seem more than you can handle on your own. There will be occasions when your anxiety worsens, and you will have frightening thoughts.

My advice to you is: **be kind to yourself, remember that you are not alone, and keep in mind that your life is worth living!**

THANK YOU for taking the time to read this book. I hope that my journey to self-healing inspires you to move forward with yours.

I wish you nothing but a happy life.

"Smile, breathe, and go slowly."

- Thich Nhat Hanh

Review Request

If you enjoyed this book or found it useful I'd like to ask you for a quick favor:

Please share your thoughts and leave a quick review.

Your feedback matters and helps me make improvements to provide the best content possible.

Reviews are incredibly helpful to both readers and authors like me, so any help would be greatly appreciated.

You can leave a review here by scanning the QR code:

Also, please join my ARC team to get early access to my preleases.

THANK YOU!

Further Reading

DBT Workbook For Teens:

A Complete Dialectical Behavior Therapy Toolkit

Essential Coping Skills and Practical Activities To Help Teenagers & Adolescents Manage Stress, Anxiety, ADHD, Phobias & More

Get it here:

https://tinyurl.com/dbt-teens

DBT Workbook For Kids:

Fun & Practical Dialectal Behavior Therapy Skills Training For Children

Help Kids Recognize Their Emotions, Manage Anxiety & Phobias, and Learn To Thrive!

Get it here:

https://tinyurl.com/dbtkids

About the Author

Barrett Huang is an author and businessman. Barrett spent years discovering the best ways to manage his OCD, overcome his anxiety, and learn to embrace life. Through his writing, he hopes to share his knowledge with readers, empowering people of all backgrounds with the tools and strategies they need to improve their mental wellbeing and be happy and healthy.

When not writing or running his business, Barrett loves to spend his time studying. He holds a University degree in Psychology. Barrett's idol is Bruce Lee, who said, "The key to immortality is first living a life worth remembering."

Learn more about Barrett's books here:
https://barretthuang.com/

Glossary

Acute Stress Disorder

A condition characterized by a powerful and unpleasant reaction that develops in the weeks following a traumatic event.

Attention Deficit Hyperactivity Disorder (ADHD)

A long-lasting disorder that affects a person's capacity to focus, sit still, and control behavior.

Borderline Personality Disorder (BPD)

A condition characterized by a person's inability to regulate emotions.

Cognitive Behavior Therapy (CBT)

A form of psychological treatment aims to reduce symptoms of various mental health conditions, primarily depression and anxiety disorders.

Complex PTSD (C-PTSD)

A condition in which you have some PTSD symptoms and some extra symptoms, such as difficulties controlling your emotions, feeling enraged, or being distrustful of the world.

Dialectical Behavior Therapy (BDT)

A modified type of cognitive-behavior therapy that's been specially adapted for people who feel emotions intensely.

Eye Movement Desensitization and Reprocessing (EMDR)

A form of psychotherapy developed by Francine Shapiro in the 1980s. A person receiving EMDR treatment is asked to recall troubling experiences while doing bilateral stimulation, such as side-to-side eye movement.

Generalized Anxiety Disorder (GAD)

A condition characterized by persistent worrying or anxiety about several areas that are out of proportion to the impact of the events.

Learned Helplessness

A phenomenon in which people believe they cannot change their situation after repeatedly experiencing a traumatic event.

Learned Optimism

The practice of learning to recognize and fight negative ideas and replacing them with positive ones.

Obsessive-Compulsive Disorder (OCD)

A condition in which people have recurring, unwanted thoughts, ideas, or sensations (obsessions) that make them feel driven to do something repetitively (compulsions).

Obsessive-Compulsive Disorder (OCD)

A condition wherein a person has uncontrollable, recurring thoughts (obsessions) and/or behaviors (compulsions) that they feel compelled to repeat.

Panic Attack

A brief period of extreme fear that results in strong physical symptoms despite the absence of any real danger or apparent cause.

Panic Disorder

An anxiety disorder characterized by sudden and recurring bouts of great fear, which may go with physical symptoms such as chest pains, heart tremors, panting, vertigo, or gastrointestinal problems.

Phobia

Anxiety or aversion to something excessive or unjustified.

Post-Traumatic Stress Disorder (PTSD)

A disorder that progresses in some people after witnessing a shocking, frightening, or dangerous event.

Social Anxiety Disorder

A condition characterized by an intense and persistent fear of being observed and judged by others.

Index

References

1 LaFreniere, L. S., & Newman, M. G. (2020). Exposing worry's deceit: Percentage of untrue worries in generalized anxiety disorder treatment. *Behavior Therapy, 51*(3), 413–423. https://doi.org/10.1016/j.beth.2019.07.003

2 Linehan, M. (2021). Building a Life Worth Living: A Memoir. Random House.

3 Mayo Foundation for Medical Education and Research. (2021, July 8). *Chronic stress puts your health at risk*. Mayo Clinic. Retrieved April 18, 2022, from https://www.mayoclinic.org/healthy-lifestyle/stress-management/in-depth/stress/art-20046037

4 Ritschel, L. A., Lim, N. E., & Stewart, L. M. (2015). Transdiagnostic applications of DBT for adolescents and adults. *American Journal of Psychotherapy, 69*(2), 111–128. https://doi.org/10.1176/appi.psychotherapy.2015.69.2.111

5 Groth, A. (2012, July 24). *You're the average of the five people you spend the most time with*. Business Insider. Retrieved April 21, 2022, from https://www.businessinsider.com/jim-rohn-youre-the-average-of-the-five-people-you-spend-the-most-time-with-2012-7

6 Pourjali, F., & Zarnaghash, M. (2010). Relationships between assertiveness and the power of saying no with mental health among undergraduate student. *Procedia - Social and Behavioral Sciences, 9*, 137–141. https://doi.org/10.1016/j.sbspro.2010.12.126

7 Kedia, G., Mussweiler, T., & Linden, D. E. J. (2014). Brain mechanisms of social comparison and their influence on the reward system. *NeuroReport, 25*(16), 1255–1265. https://doi.org/10.1097/wnr.0000000000000255

8 Karim, F., Oyewande, A., Abdalla, L. F., Chaudhry Ehsanullah, R., & Khan, S. (2020). Social media use and its connection to Mental Health: A Systematic Review. *Cureus*. https://doi.org/10.7759/cureus.8627

9 Ouellette, C. (2020, December 23). *FOMO statistics you need to grow your business*. TrustPulse. Retrieved April 2022, from https://trustpulse.com/fomo-statistics/

10 Bressan, R. A., & Crippa, J. A. (2005). The role of dopamine in reward and pleasure behaviour - review of data from Preclinical Research. *Acta Psychiatrica Scandinavica, 111*(s427), 14–21. https://doi.org/10.1111/j.1600-0447.2005.00540.x

11 Houlis, A. M. (n.d.). *5 things successful people do when setting boundaries at work*. Fairygodboss. Retrieved April 2, 2022, from https://fairygodboss.com/career-topics/setting-boundaries-at-work

12 Marie, O. (2020, November 28). *5 things science tells us about morning routine*. Science Times. Retrieved April 2, 2022, from https://www.sciencetimes.com/articles/28438/20201128/5-things-science-tells-morning-routine.htm

13 P., S. M. E. (2006). *Learned optimism how to change your mind and your life; with a new preface*. Vintage Books.

14 Scheier, M. F., & Carver, C. S. (1992). Effects of optimism on psychological and physical well-being: Theoretical overview and empirical update. *Cognitive Therapy and Research, 16*(2), 201–228. https://doi.org/10.1007/bf01173489

15 Rasmussen, H. N., Scheier, M. F., & Greenhouse, J. B. (2009). Optimism and physical health: A meta-analytic review. *Annals of Behavioral Medicine, 37*(3), 239–256. https://doi.org/10.1007/s12160-009-9111-x

16 Allen , V. L. (2017). Learned Optimism: A Balm for Social Worker Stress. *Social Work & Christianity, 44*(4), 83–91. https://doi.org/10.34043/swc.v46i2

17 Achor, S. (2018). *The happiness advantage: How a positive brain fuels success in work and life.* Currency.

18 Davidson, R. J., & Lutz, A. (2008). Buddha's brain: Neuroplasticity and meditation [in the spotlight]. *IEEE Signal Processing Magazine, 25*(1), 176–174. https://doi.org/10.1109/msp.2008.4431873

19 Davidson, R. J., Kabat-Zinn, J., Schumacher, J., Rosenkranz, M., Muller, D., Santorelli, S. F., Urbanowski, F., Harrington, A., Bonus, K., & Sheridan, J. F. (2003). Alterations in brain and immune function produced by mindfulness meditation. *Psychosomatic Medicine, 65*(4), 564–570. https://doi.org/10.1097/01.psy.0000077505.67574.e3

20 Hölzel, B. K., Carmody, J., Vangel, M., Congleton, C., Yerramsetti, S. M., Gard, T., & Lazar, S. W. (2011). Mindfulness practice leads to increases in regional brain gray matter density. *Psychiatry Research: Neuroimaging, 191*(1), 36–43. https://doi.org/10.1016/j.pscychresns.2010.08.006

21 Hofmann, S. G., & Gómez, A. F. (2017). Mindfulness-based interventions for anxiety and depression. *Psychiatric Clinics of North America, 40*(4), 739–749. https://doi.org/10.1016/j.psc.2017.08.008

22 Shapiro, E. and D. (2017, May 23). *The difference between mindfulness and meditation.* Medium. Retrieved April 2, 2022, from https://medium.com/thrive-global/mindfulness-meditation-whats-the-difference-852f5ef7ec1a#

23 Basso, J. C., McHale, A., Ende, V., Oberlin, D. J., & Suzuki, W. A. (2019). Brief, daily meditation enhances attention, memory, mood, and emotional regulation in non-experienced meditators. *Behavioural Brain Research, 356*, 208–220. https://doi.org/10.1016/j.bbr.2018.08.023

24 Fayyad, J., Sampson, N. A., Hwang, I., Adamowski, T., Aguilar-Gaxiola, S., Al-Hamzawi, A., Andrade, L. H., Borges, G., de Girolamo, G., Florescu, S., Gureje, O., Haro, J. M., Hu, C., Karam, E. G., Lee, S., Navarro-Mateu, F., O'Neill, S., Pennell, B.-E., Piazza, M., … Kessler, R. C. (2016). The descriptive epidemiology of DSM-IV ADULT ADHD in the World Health Organization World Mental Health Surveys. *ADHD Attention Deficit and Hyperactivity Disorders, 9*(1), 47–65. https://doi.org/10.1007/s12402-016-0208-3

25 Fuller-Thomson, E., Lewis, D. A., & Agbeyaka, S. (2021). Attention-deficit/hyperactivity disorder and alcohol and other substance use disorders in young adulthood: Findings from a Canadian Nationally Representative survey. *Alcohol and Alcoholism.* https://doi.org/10.1093/alcalc/agab048

26 Molina BSG;Pelham WE;Cheong J;Marshal MP;Gnagy EM;Curran PJ; (n.d.). Childhood attention-deficit/hyperactivity disorder (ADHD) and growth in adolescent alcohol use: The roles of functional impairments, ADHD symptom persistence, and parental knowledge. Journal of abnormal psychology. Retrieved April 30, 2022, from https://pubmed.ncbi.nlm.nih.gov/22845650/

27 U.S. Department of Health and Human Services. (n.d.). *Specific phobia.* National Institute of Mental Health. Retrieved April 2, 2022, from https://www.nimh.nih.gov/health/statistics/specific-phobia

28 Becker, C. B., & Zayfert, C. (2001). Integrating DBT-based techniques and concepts to facilitate exposure treatment for PTSD. *Cognitive and Behavioral Practice, 8*(2), 107–122. https://doi.org/10.1016/s1077-7229(01)80017-1

29 Bohus, M., Kleindienst, N., Hahn, C., Müller-Engelmann, M., Ludäscher, P., Steil, R., Fydrich, T., Kuehner, C., Resick, P. A., Stiglmayr, C., Schmahl, C.,

& Priebe, K. (2020). Dialectical behavior therapy for posttraumatic stress disorder (DBT-PTSD) compared with Cognitive Processing Therapy (CPT) in complex presentations of PTSD in women survivors of childhood abuse. *JAMA Psychiatry, 77*(12), 1235. https://doi.org/10.1001/jamapsychiatry.2020.2148

30 Pally, R. (1998). Emotional processing: The mind-body connection. *International Journal of Psycho-Analysis, 79*, 349-362.

31 Schwartz, J., & Beyette, B. (2016). *Brain Lock: Free Yourself From Obsessive-Compulsive Behavior: A Four-Step Self-Treatment Method To Change Your Brain Chemistry*. Harper Perennial.

32 *Facts & Statistics: Anxiety and Depression Association of America, ADAA.* Facts & Statistics | Anxiety and Depression Association of America, ADAA. (n.d.). Retrieved April 2, 2022, from https://adaa.org/understanding-anxiety/facts-statistics

33 Miller, T. W., & Kraus, R. F. (2007). Modified dialectical behavior therapy and problem solving for obsessive-compulsive personality disorder. *Journal of Contemporary Psychotherapy, 37*(2), 79–85. https://doi.org/10.1007/s10879-006-9039-4

34 Ahovan, M., Balali, S., Abedi Shargh, N., & Doostian, Y. (2016). Efficacy of dialectical behavior therapy on clinical signs and emotion regulation in patients with obsessive-compulsive disorder. *Mediterranean Journal of Social Sciences.* https://doi.org/10.5901/mjss.2016.v7n4p412

35 Shameli, L., Mehrabizadeh Honarmand, M., Naa'mi, A., & Davodi, I. (2019). The effectiveness of emotion-focused therapy on emotion regulation styles and severity of obsessive-compulsive symptoms in women with obsessive-compulsive disorder. *Iranian Journal of Psychiatry and Clinical Psychology*, 356–369. https://doi.org/10.32598/ijpcp.24.4.456

36 Hirshkowitz, M., Whiton, K., Albert, S. M., Alessi, C., Bruni, O., DonCarlos, L., Hazen, N., Herman, J., Katz, E. S., Kheirandish-Gozal, L., Neubauer, D. N., O'Donnell, A. E., Ohayon, M., Peever, J., Rawding, R., Sachdeva, R. C., Setters, B., Vitiello, M. V., Ware, J. C., & Adams Hillard, P. J. (2015). National Sleep Foundation's sleep time duration recommendations: Methodology and results summary. *Sleep Health*, *1*(1), 40–43. https://doi.org/10.1016/j.sleh.2014.12.010

37 Akbaraly, T. N., Brunner, E. J., Ferrie, J. E., Marmot, M. G., Kivimaki, M., & Singh-Manoux, A. (2009). Dietary pattern and depressive symptoms in middle age. *British Journal of Psychiatry*, *195*(5), 408–413. https://doi.org/10.1192/bjp.bp.108.058925

38 MD, E. S. (2020, March 26). *Nutritional psychiatry: Your brain on food*. Harvard Health. Retrieved April 3, 2022, from https://www.health.harvard.edu/blog/nutritional-psychiatry-your-brain-on-food-201511168626

39 Parker, G. B., Brotchie, H., & Graham, R. K. (2017). Vitamin D and depression. *Journal of Affective Disorders*, *208*, 56–61. https://doi.org/10.1016/j.jad.2016.08.082

40 Plevin, D., & Galletly, C. (2020). The neuropsychiatric effects of vitamin C deficiency: A systematic review. *BMC Psychiatry*, *20*(1). https://doi.org/10.1186/s12888-020-02730-w

41 White, D., Cox, K., Peters, R., Pipingas, A., & Scholey, A. (2015). Effects of four-week supplementation with a multi-vitamin/mineral preparation on mood and blood biomarkers in young adults: A randomised, double-blind, placebo-controlled trial. *Nutrients, 7*(11), 9005–9017. https://doi.org/10.3390/nu7115451

42 Long, S.-J., & Benton, D. (2013). Effects of vitamin and mineral supplementation on stress, mild psychiatric symptoms, and mood in nonclinical samples. *Psychosomatic Medicine, 75*(2), 144–153. https://doi.org/10.1097/psy.0b013e31827d5fbd

43 Su, K.-P., Tseng, P.-T., Lin, P.-Y., Okubo, R., Chen, T.-Y., Chen, Y.-W., & Matsuoka, Y. J. (2018). Association of use of omega-3 polyunsaturated fatty acids with changes in severity of anxiety symptoms. *JAMA Network Open, 1*(5). https://doi.org/10.1001/jamanetworkopen.2018.2327

Made in the USA
Coppell, TX
13 October 2022

84574717R00096